SQUIRREL MONKEY

The Complete Guide To Squirrel Monkey Ownership, Care, And Conservation: Understanding Behavior, Legalities, Housing, Health, Diet, and Lifelong Companionship.

BY

GEORGE UNITY

COPYRIGHT © 2025 ALL RIGHT RESERVED

TABLE OF CONTENTS

CHAPTER 1:
INTRODUCTION TO SQUIRREL MONKEYS

CHAPTER 2:
SPECIES AND SUBSPECIES OF SQUIRREL MONKEYS

CHAPTER 3:
NATURAL HISTORY AND BEHAVIOR OF SQUIRREL MONKEYS

CHAPTER 4:
LEGAL CONSIDERATIONS AND ETHICAL CONCERNS OF SQUIRREL MONKEY OWNERSHIP

CHAPTER 5:
SOURCING AND ADOPTION

CHAPTER 6:
PREPARING YOUR HOME

CHAPTER 7:
DIET AND NUTRITION

CHAPTER 8:
DAILY CARE AND ENRICHMENT

CHAPTER 9:
HEALTH AND VETERINARY CARE

CHAPTER 10:
SOCIALIZATION AND BEHAVIOR MANAGEMENT

CHAPTER 11:

BREEDING AND REPRODUCTION (OPTIONAL CHAPTER FOR BREEDERS)

CHAPTER 12:
LIFESPAN, AGING, AND END-OF-LIFE CARE

CHAPTER 13:
SQUIRREL MONKEYS IN RESEARCH AND ENTERTAINMENT

CHAPTER 14:
CONSERVATION AND THE WILD POPULATION

CHAPTER 15:
RESOURCES AND NEXT STEPS

CHAPTER 1:

INTRODUCTION TO SQUIRREL MONKEYS

Squirrel monkeys are among the most captivating and intriguing members of the primate world. With their expressive eyes, quick movements, and social intelligence, they have earned a place in the hearts of animal lovers and researchers alike. These tiny yet spirited monkeys embody a unique blend of curiosity, energy, and beauty, making them stand out even in the diverse primate family. In this chapter, we explore the fundamental details about squirrel monkeys, including their scientific classification, natural distribution, and why they continue to captivate both the scientific community and the general public. We also critically assess their suitability as exotic pets, an issue that continues to generate both interest and controversy.

Overview of the Species (Scientific Name and Classification)

Squirrel monkeys belong to the genus Saimiri, which is part of the Cebidae family in the order Primates. They are classified under the suborder Haplorhini, which includes tarsiers, monkeys, and apes. Within the Saimiri genus, several distinct species have been identified, including Saimiri sciureus (the common squirrel monkey), Saimiri boliviensis (the Bolivian squirrel monkey), and Saimiri ustus (the bare-eared squirrel monkey), among others.

Though they share many similarities, squirrel monkeys exhibit slight differences in coloration, size, and geographic distribution. Their classification has undergone numerous revisions over the decades, as taxonomists have debated the validity of various subspecies and species distinctions. The advent of molecular genetics and DNA analysis has helped clarify many of these relationships, although new research continues to reshape our understanding of the Saimiri genus.

Squirrel monkeys are considered part of the New World monkeys, a group that includes capuchins, howler monkeys, and tamarins, all native to Central and South America. New World monkeys are characterized by their flat noses, long tails (often prehensile in some species), and arboreal lifestyles. Squirrel monkeys differ from their larger primate cousins by being much smaller, weighing only 600 to 1,100 grams (approximately 1.3 to 2.4 pounds) and measuring about 25 to 35 centimeters in body length, with tails that can be even longer than their bodies. Their tails, however, are not prehensile but are used for balance as they leap and navigate through the treetops.

These monkeys have relatively large brains for their body size, which contributes to their high levels of intelligence and complex social behaviors. Their facial features are often described as "doll-like," with bright, expressive eyes and a distinctive black-and-white facial mask. This unique combination of appearance and personality has played a significant role in their popularity both in zoos and private collections.

Origin and Natural Habitats

Squirrel monkeys are native to the tropical forests of Central and South America. Their range extends from Costa Rica in Central America to the Amazon basin in Brazil, Bolivia, Colombia, Ecuador, French Guiana, Guyana, Peru, Suriname, and Venezuela. Each species and subspecies occupies a particular ecological niche within this expansive range, adapting to the unique conditions of their local habitats.

These monkeys thrive in dense, humid rainforests, especially along riverbanks and in secondary forests where the canopy allows for a multi-tiered arboreal lifestyle. They prefer the middle and lower canopy layers, where they can easily forage for fruits, insects, and small vertebrates. Their agility and small size allow them to dart quickly between branches and vines, a necessity given the number of natural predators they face, including snakes, birds of prey, and wild cats.

Squirrel monkeys are diurnal, meaning they are active during the day and rest at night. Their daily lives involve social interactions within their troop, which can range from 10 to over 100 individuals. These groups are structured according to age, sex, and dominance, and they exhibit coordinated movements and cooperative behaviors while foraging and defending territory.

The rainforest provides not only their food but also essential cover from predators and temperature extremes. However, squirrel monkeys are increasingly threatened by habitat destruction due to logging, agriculture, and urbanization. In some regions, they are also captured for the illegal pet trade or used in biomedical research.

Despite these threats, several species of squirrel monkeys remain relatively stable in population, though others are listed as near-threatened or vulnerable by conservation organizations.

Why They Fascinate People

Squirrel monkeys have fascinated humans for centuries, not only because of their appealing appearance but also due to their complex behaviors, intelligence, and emotional expressiveness. From indigenous communities in South America who regarded them with reverence or curiosity, to modern-day researchers and pet owners, these monkeys have consistently inspired awe and admiration.

One of the most captivating aspects of squirrel monkeys is their liveliness. They move with speed and precision through the treetops, exhibiting impressive agility and coordination. Observing a troop of squirrel monkeys in the wild is akin to watching a well-rehearsed acrobatic performance; their movements are swift, synchronized, and seemingly effortless. This level of physical skill is especially appealing to those who study animal locomotion or design enrichment activities in captive environments.

Equally fascinating is their social structure. Squirrel monkeys communicate through a complex system of vocalizations, facial expressions, and body language. They use different calls to warn each other of predators, indicate food sources, or maintain contact while moving through dense vegetation. Researchers studying animal communication have been particularly intrigued by their vocal repertoire and its potential parallels with the early stages of human language development.

Their cognitive abilities further enhance their appeal. Squirrel monkeys are capable of learning through observation, problem-solving, and memory retention. In captivity, they can be trained to perform simple tasks, recognize symbols, and manipulate tools. These skills make them a favorite subject in neurological and psychological studies, though such use has raised ethical concerns over time.

From a purely emotional standpoint, their expressive faces and curious eyes evoke a sense of kinship and empathy in humans. Many people find it difficult to look at a squirrel monkey and not feel some degree of emotional connection, which has contributed to their popularity as exotic pets, zoo animals, and even media icons. However, this very fascination also leads to complicated consequences when people attempt to domesticate them without fully understanding their needs.

Suitability as Exotic Pets

Despite their appeal, squirrel monkeys are not ideal pets for the average person. Owning a squirrel monkey comes with a wide range of responsibilities, challenges, and ethical implications that must be carefully considered. While some individuals may have the resources and experience to care for such a demanding animal, most are unprepared for the level of commitment required.

First and foremost, squirrel monkeys are highly social animals. In the wild, they live in large, dynamic groups and rely heavily on social interactions for mental stimulation and emotional wellbeing. Isolating a squirrel monkey from its peers—especially in a home environment—can lead to psychological distress, depression, and behavioral issues such as aggression or self-harm. Keeping a single monkey without sufficient enrichment, attention, or companionship is widely regarded as inhumane.

Additionally, these primates are incredibly intelligent and require constant mental and physical stimulation. Boredom can quickly lead to destructive behaviors. They can dismantle cages, escape from enclosures, and even damage household items if given the opportunity. Unlike dogs or cats, squirrel monkeys do not respond well to traditional obedience training, and their instincts often clash with human expectations of pet behavior.

Their dietary needs are another challenge. Squirrel monkeys require a varied and carefully balanced diet, which includes fresh fruits, vegetables, insects, and specialized primate supplements. Improper nutrition can result in severe health problems such as metabolic bone disease, obesity, or malnutrition. Regular veterinary care is essential, yet finding a vet with experience in primate health can be both difficult and costly.

Moreover, squirrel monkeys can carry zoonotic diseases—illnesses that can be transmitted between animals and humans. These include herpes B virus, salmonella, and other infectious agents. While the risk is relatively low with proper hygiene and care, it is still a concern for families with children, the elderly, or immunocompromised individuals.

Legal considerations also play a major role. In many countries and U.S. states, it is either illegal to own a squirrel monkey or heavily regulated. Prospective owners may need to obtain permits, meet strict enclosure standards, and submit to routine inspections. Failing to comply with these laws can result in fines, confiscation of the animal, or worse.

Ethically, the exotic pet trade raises serious concerns. Many squirrel monkeys are captured from the wild or bred in substandard conditions. Even in reputable breeding programs, separating infants from their mothers too early or selling them to inexperienced owners can result in lasting trauma. Advocacy groups argue that keeping such intelligent, social creatures in private homes is inherently exploitative, no matter how well-intentioned the owner.

Nevertheless, there are exceptions. Some individuals or facilities—such as licensed sanctuaries, zoological parks, or researchers—may provide an environment that meets the monkeys' complex needs. In these controlled settings, squirrel monkeys can thrive, provided they receive proper nutrition, medical care, companionship, and environmental enrichment.

In conclusion, while squirrel monkeys are undeniably fascinating and beautiful creatures, their suitability as exotic pets is limited to a very narrow set of circumstances. For most people, the challenges of providing adequate care, meeting legal obligations, and ensuring ethical treatment far outweigh the novelty or joy of ownership. Instead, appreciating squirrel monkeys in sanctuaries, conservation centers, or educational settings is a more sustainable and humane way to engage with these remarkable primates.

CHAPTER 2:

SPECIES AND SUBSPECIES OF SQUIRREL MONKEYS

Squirrel monkeys are a remarkable genus of small primates scientifically known as Saimiri. These monkeys are among the most agile and intelligent of the New World primates and are characterized by their expressive faces, fast movements, and complex social structures. Though often generalized under the umbrella term "squirrel monkey," the genus Saimiri includes multiple species and subspecies, each with its own unique behaviors, appearances, and ecological preferences. Understanding the differences between these species is essential not only for conservation efforts but also for responsible ownership and care in captivity.

In this chapter, we will explore the major species and subspecies of squirrel monkeys, their behavioral and physical distinctions, habitat preferences, and which among them are most commonly found in zoological collections, research institutions, and, less commonly, private ownership.

An Overview of the Genus Saimiri

The genus Saimiri falls within the family Cebidae, which also includes capuchins. All squirrel monkeys are native to Central and South America, and their collective range extends from Costa Rica in the north to Brazil and Bolivia in the south. These monkeys are diurnal, arboreal, and extremely social. Their genus name, Saimiri, is derived from indigenous South American languages, referencing their nimble and lively behavior.

Despite being relatively small primates, squirrel monkeys have large brains in proportion to their body size. This neurological advantage manifests in their problem-solving skills, memory, and social communication. However, different species of Saimiri exhibit variations in these behaviors and traits depending on their specific ecological environments.

Currently, taxonomists generally recognize around five primary species of squirrel monkeys, with several additional subspecies. These include:

1. Saimiri sciureus – Common Squirrel Monkey
2. Saimiri boliviensis – Bolivian Squirrel Monkey
3. Saimiri oerstedii – Central American Squirrel Monkey
4. Saimiri ustus – Bare-eared Squirrel Monkey
5. Saimiri vanzolinii – Black-headed Squirrel Monkey

Each species exhibits unique features that distinguish it from the others, ranging from facial coloration to geographic distribution.

1. Saimiri sciureus – Common Squirrel Monkey

The common squirrel monkey is perhaps the most recognized member of the Saimiri genus and was once believed to encompass several subspecies. It is native to the Amazon basin, primarily found in Brazil, Colombia, and parts of Venezuela. They are adaptable to various forest types, including flooded forests, secondary growth, and disturbed habitats.

In terms of appearance, Saimiri sciureus is known for its bright yellow limbs, white face mask, and black mouth and nose area. Their tails are non-prehensile but long and slender, used primarily for balance. These monkeys are small, weighing around 700 to 1100 grams (1.5 to 2.4 pounds), and typically live in large, mixed-sex groups.

Behaviorally, they are extremely vocal and agile. Their diet consists of fruits, insects, small vertebrates, and nectar. In the wild, they rely on keen social coordination to forage and avoid predators. Though once common in pet trade and research, their capture from the wild is now restricted in most countries.

2. Saimiri boliviensis – Bolivian Squirrel Monkey

The Bolivian squirrel monkey, often confused with Saimiri sciureus, is found in Bolivia, southern Brazil, and Peru. It thrives in tropical rainforests and prefers humid, dense canopies with plenty of cover.

This species is distinguished by its more distinct black "cap" or crown on its head, making it easily recognizable. Unlike S. sciureus, its face is often whiter, and the mouth less dark, giving it a different expression. Behaviorally, S. boliviensis is slightly more gregarious and social, often forming larger troops than its relatives.

In captivity, Saimiri boliviensis is one of the most common species found in zoos, laboratories, and even private collections. It has been widely used in neurological and behavioral research due to its manageable size and intelligent disposition. Because it adapts relatively well to captivity when social needs are met, it is favored over other species in controlled environments.

3. Saimiri oerstedii – Central American Squirrel Monkey

Native to Costa Rica and Panama, Saimiri oerstedii is perhaps the most endangered of the squirrel monkeys. Its populations have declined significantly due to deforestation, hunting, and the illegal pet trade. Unlike other squirrel monkeys, it is geographically isolated in Central America, making it ecologically and genetically distinct.

Visually, S. oerstedii has a grizzled back with a mix of reddish, gray, and black tones. Its limbs are orange or yellowish, and the facial features are more muted than its South American cousins. In the wild, it inhabits lowland forests and coastal zones, often moving in small groups.

Behaviorally, Saimiri oerstedii is known to be more cautious and less vocal than other squirrel monkeys. It has also demonstrated unique feeding behaviors, particularly with regard to insect foraging. Due to its endangered status and strict legal protections, this species is almost never found in private collections and is maintained only in specific conservation breeding programs or protected reserves.

4. *Saimiri ustus* – *Bare-eared Squirrel Monkey*

The bare-eared squirrel monkey is found primarily in central Brazil, in regions that include the Rio Madeira and Rio Tapajós. It is one of the least studied species within the genus and is known for the absence of external ear fur, which gives it its name.

Physically, S. ustus resembles S. sciureus but with more subtle facial markings and darker fur tones on the head and limbs. The absence of fur on the ears provides a notable distinction. Little is known about its behavior compared to other Saimiri species, although it is assumed to have similar dietary and social structures.

Due to limited studies and its restricted habitat, Saimiri ustus is rarely kept in captivity and is seldom seen outside of its natural range.

5. *Saimiri vanzolinii – Black-headed Squirrel Monkey*

One of the rarest and most geographically limited squirrel monkey species is Saimiri vanzolinii, found only in the Mamirauá Sustainable Development Reserve in Brazil. It has one of the most restricted ranges of any primate species on Earth.

This species has a distinctive black cap and facial pattern that sets it apart from other squirrel monkeys. Its conservation status is of serious concern due to habitat loss and limited geographic distribution.

Unlike more widespread squirrel monkeys, S. vanzolinii is virtually nonexistent in captivity. Conservationists focus on in-situ (on-site) protection of its habitat rather than relocation or captive breeding programs.

Behavioral and Ecological Differences

While all squirrel monkeys share core traits such as arboreal living, social grouping, and an omnivorous diet, each species has evolved behavioral differences shaped by their environments. For instance:

Group sizes vary, with Saimiri boliviensis often forming larger, tighter groups than Saimiri oerstedii.
Communication patterns may also differ. Some species have more complex vocalizations or are more responsive to visual cues.
Diet preferences can shift based on available food sources. Species in fruit-rich environments consume more fruit, while others rely more on insects or small vertebrates.

Moreover, territorial behavior, reproductive timing, and response to predators may all differ slightly based on geographic pressures.

Species Commonly Kept in Captivity

Of all the squirrel monkey species, Saimiri sciureus and Saimiri boliviensis are the most commonly found in zoos, research facilities, and occasionally private collections. Their adaptability, sociability, and manageable size make them the preferred species for captive environments.

Saimiri boliviensis is particularly favored for scientific research due to its intelligence and relatively docile temperament when acclimated to humans.
Saimiri sciureus has historically been popular in zoos and the exotic pet trade, although increasing regulations and ethical considerations have reduced its availability.

Other species like S. oerstedii, S. vanzolinii, and S. ustus are not commonly seen in captivity, either because of their endangered status or because they require highly specific environmental conditions that are difficult to replicate outside their natural range.

Conclusion

Squirrel monkeys may appear quite similar at first glance, but a deeper look reveals a diverse group of primates adapted to distinct environments across Central and South America. Each species brings its own challenges and fascinations to both conservation and captivity.

While Saimiri boliviensis and Saimiri sciureus are the most commonly kept and studied, all squirrel monkey species deserve attention for their roles in the ecosystem, their unique adaptations, and their fragile status in a world where their habitats are shrinking. Understanding these differences is not only vital for scientific classification and conservation but also for anyone considering the ethics and responsibilities of interacting with or keeping squirrel monkeys in any capacity.

CHAPTER 3:

NATURAL HISTORY AND BEHAVIOR OF SQUIRREL MONKEYS

Squirrel monkeys (Saimiri spp.) are among the most socially dynamic, behaviorally complex, and ecologically significant primates in the Neotropics. Native to Central and South America, these small monkeys thrive in diverse forested habitats where they display intricate social behaviors, highly adaptable foraging strategies, and advanced cognitive capabilities. Understanding their natural history is essential for anyone seeking to appreciate these remarkable primates—whether for academic, conservation, or ethical pet ownership reasons.

This chapter explores the squirrel monkey's social structure in the wild, their foraging habits and diet, the depth of their communication and intelligence, and their ecological role within their native environments.

Social Structure in the Wild

Squirrel monkeys are intensely social animals, forming large, dynamic groups known as troops. These troops can range from 10 to over 100 individuals, although the most common group size falls somewhere between 20 and 50. This group-living structure provides numerous survival benefits, including enhanced predator detection, better access to resources, and greater social learning opportunities.

Within a squirrel monkey troop, the structure is generally matrilineal, meaning females remain in their natal groups while males disperse upon reaching sexual maturity. This leads to troops where all adult females are related, creating strong matrilineal bonds. Males, especially during the non-breeding season, often exist on the periphery of the troop or travel in loose bachelor groups before attempting to integrate into a new troop.

The social dynamics among squirrel monkeys are complex and highly fluid. Dominance hierarchies are present, particularly among males during the breeding season. At this time, males become more aggressive, and their physical appearance changes—most notably, they gain weight in their upper bodies and shoulders, a condition referred to as "fattening." This temporary transformation is linked to hormonal changes and is an indicator of social and reproductive readiness. The heaviest, most dominant males typically gain greater access to fertile females.

Female squirrel monkeys, while less overtly aggressive, maintain hierarchies of their own. These social rankings influence grooming partnerships, foraging privileges, and the level of social support an individual might receive during conflicts or stress.

Social behaviors in squirrel monkeys include grooming, play, vocal communication, coordinated movement, and cooperative defense against predators. Juvenile monkeys engage in frequent play, which includes chasing, wrestling, and mock-fighting. Such play not only strengthens social bonds but also helps young monkeys develop the skills necessary for adult life.

In the wild, troops are cohesive yet flexible. They may split temporarily into subgroups during foraging or when resources are scarce—a behavior known as fission-fusion dynamics. Despite occasional separation, the monkeys rely on continuous vocalizations to stay in touch and reunite quickly.

Foraging Habits and Diet

Squirrel monkeys are opportunistic omnivores with a highly adaptable foraging strategy. Their diet varies depending on the season, local habitat, and available food sources. Primarily, their food intake consists of fruits, insects, nectar, small vertebrates (such as lizards and tree frogs), seeds, flowers, and other plant parts.

Fruits make up the largest portion of their diet during the wet season when they are most abundant. These monkeys have evolved to be highly frugivorous during such times, consuming a wide array of soft, pulpy fruits, many of which are found in the mid to lower canopy. Insects, however, become particularly important in the dry season or when fruit is scarce. Protein-rich arthropods, including grasshoppers, spiders, beetles, and caterpillars, are actively hunted by individuals or small subgroups.

Squirrel monkeys are also known to forage for nectar and sap, playing an indirect role in pollination. Their dexterous hands and keen eyesight enable them to locate and extract these resources efficiently. Additionally, their feeding patterns often overlap with other primate species such as capuchins or howler monkeys. In fact, squirrel monkeys are known to associate with capuchins in mixed-species groups, likely because capuchins help locate food and deter predators.

These monkeys are diurnal foragers, meaning they are active during the day and rest at night. A typical foraging expedition involves coordinated movements through the canopy as the troop searches for ripe fruit trees or insect-rich foliage. Squirrel monkeys rely on memory and spatial navigation to return to previously fruitful feeding sites, showcasing their cognitive mapping abilities.

Foraging is not just a solitary effort but a highly social activity. Individuals watch each other closely and will often follow companions who seem to have found food. However, competition can be intense, particularly during periods of scarcity. Dominant individuals may have first access to choice food items, and lower-ranking monkeys may resort to stealth or distraction techniques to secure their share.

The diversity in their diet makes squirrel monkeys important for seed dispersal. As they consume fruits and excrete seeds across wide areas, they contribute to forest regeneration and plant biodiversity. Their insectivory, on the other hand, helps regulate arthropod populations, adding to their ecological value.

Communication and Intelligence

Squirrel monkeys possess an impressive range of vocalizations, body postures, facial expressions, and olfactory signals, all of which contribute to their intricate communication system. These tools are crucial for coordinating group movements, reinforcing social bonds, alerting others to danger, and establishing dominance or submission.

Vocal communication is perhaps the most striking feature of squirrel monkey behavior. They produce dozens of different calls, including:

Alarm calls to warn of aerial or terrestrial predators

Contact calls to maintain troop cohesion

Distress calls from juveniles or separated individuals

Aggressive or submissive vocalizations during social disputes

Their calls vary in pitch, frequency, and duration, and some have distinct meanings depending on context. For example, a "chuck" or "peep" call might signal mild agitation or curiosity, while a high-pitched scream could indicate a serious threat or injury.

Visual communication also plays a significant role. Facial expressions—such as the opening of the mouth, raising of eyebrows, or narrowing of the eyes—can signal aggression, submission, or contentment. Tail postures, such as arching or flicking, are used in social interactions or during vigilance.

Olfactory cues, including urine washing (rubbing urine on hands and feet), play roles in territorial marking, reproductive signaling, and social identification. These behaviors are especially common among males during the mating season, helping to attract females or deter rivals.

Beyond communication, squirrel monkeys are remarkably intelligent. They demonstrate advanced problem-solving skills, object manipulation, tool use in rare cases, and social learning. In laboratory settings, squirrel monkeys have been trained to use levers, recognize patterns, and even discriminate between numerical quantities.

Their intelligence is evident in the wild as well. They remember food locations, understand relationships between group members, and alter their behaviors based on context. For example, mothers teach their offspring which insects are safe to eat by modeling and guiding behavior, a clear sign of cultural transmission.

Juveniles learn social cues and foraging strategies through observation and mimicry, reflecting the cognitive plasticity of the species. They also engage in strategic play, which develops both motor and social skills.

Role in Their Native Ecosystem

Squirrel monkeys play several critical roles in the ecosystems of Central and South America. As omnivorous foragers, they influence plant regeneration, insect populations, and even the health of the forests they inhabit.

One of their most significant ecological functions is seed dispersal. When eating fruit, squirrel monkeys ingest seeds and later defecate them in new locations, often far from the parent tree. This not only helps in plant propagation but also reduces competition for resources near the original tree. Their frequent movement through the forest means they disperse seeds widely, contributing to plant diversity and forest regeneration.

Insect predation is another important ecological service. By consuming vast numbers of insects, especially during the dry season, squirrel monkeys help regulate pest populations. Their targeted hunting of certain insect groups may influence the dynamics of the forest arthropod community, helping maintain a balance that supports overall ecosystem health.

Their interaction with other species—such as mixed-species foraging groups—enhances biodiversity and creates complex interspecies networks. Squirrel monkeys may act as sentinels for capuchins or vice versa, depending on the situation. Such cooperation increases vigilance against predators and improves foraging efficiency.

Additionally, squirrel monkeys serve as prey for a variety of predators, including snakes, hawks, jaguars, and ocelots. Their position as both predator and prey makes them a vital link in the food web. Their behaviors—such as alarm calling or mobbing threats—can even influence the behavior of other species in the area, creating ripple effects throughout the ecosystem.

Unfortunately, the very traits that make squirrel monkeys ecologically important also make them vulnerable. Habitat fragmentation, logging, and urban development destroy the interconnected canopy networks they rely on. Road construction and deforestation reduce their range and force them into smaller, isolated populations. When food becomes scarce due to environmental degradation, even their robust foraging strategies may not suffice.

Efforts to protect squirrel monkeys—especially through the establishment of protected areas, wildlife corridors, and reforestation—are not just about saving a single species. They are about preserving the integrity of an entire ecosystem where countless plants, animals, and microorganisms interact in delicate balance.

Conclusion

Squirrel monkeys are small but mighty players in the ecological tapestry of the Neotropics. Their complex social systems, versatile diets, communicative intelligence, and ecological contributions reflect an evolutionary lineage that has finely adapted to life in the treetops.

Understanding their natural history is more than an academic exercise—it is a foundation for ethical care, informed conservation, and respectful coexistence. Whether swinging through the canopy in dense Amazonian forests or living under human care in reputable sanctuaries, squirrel monkeys exemplify the beauty, intelligence, and fragility of the natural world.

As stewards of biodiversity, we owe these incredible creatures not just admiration, but protection. In the chapters ahead, we will examine both the challenges and responsibilities that come with sharing our world—and sometimes our homes—with squirrel monkeys.

CHAPTER 4:

LEGAL CONSIDERATIONS AND ETHICAL CONCERNS OF SQUIRREL MONKEY OWNERSHIP

Squirrel monkeys, with their expressive faces, intelligent eyes, and captivating behaviors, often attract admiration and fascination. However, the idea of keeping a squirrel monkey as a pet is far more complicated than many people realize. While some envision bonding with these lively primates in a household setting, the reality involves a tangled web of legal restrictions, ethical debates, and complex responsibilities. Understanding these legal and moral dimensions is critical not only for potential owners but also for policymakers, conservationists, and the general public.

This chapter explores the laws and regulations governing squirrel monkey ownership around the world, the types of permits and licensing required, the deeper ethical implications of keeping primates as pets, and the significant responsibilities that come with exotic pet ownership.

Laws and Regulations on Owning Squirrel Monkeys (By Region/Country)

The legality of owning squirrel monkeys as pets varies widely depending on the country, state, or even local jurisdiction. These laws are often influenced by public safety concerns, conservation goals, animal welfare ethics, and environmental impact. In many regions, squirrel monkeys fall under the broader category of exotic or non-human primates, which are subject to strict regulations.

In the United States, the legal landscape is patchy and inconsistent. While there is no overarching federal law explicitly banning the ownership of squirrel monkeys as pets, several important federal regulations apply. The U.S. Department of Agriculture (USDA) regulates individuals who breed, sell, or exhibit primates under the Animal Welfare Act. Private owners may be subject to USDA inspections if they meet certain thresholds, such as breeding for sale or displaying the animal to the public.

At the state level, laws vary dramatically:

Some states such as California, New York, and New Jersey have outright bans on private primate ownership, including squirrel monkeys.

Others like Texas, Florida, and Nevada allow ownership but require special permits or adherence to zoning regulations.

A few states have little to no restrictions, but local ordinances may still apply.

In Canada, squirrel monkey ownership is typically regulated at the provincial and municipal level. Provinces such as Ontario and British Columbia may permit ownership, but major cities like Toronto or Vancouver often prohibit it. Enforcement is usually tied to public health, animal welfare, and community safety.

In the United Kingdom, private ownership of squirrel monkeys is legal under certain conditions, but highly regulated. The Dangerous Wild Animals Act 1976 requires individuals to obtain a license from their local authority. Applicants must prove they can meet housing, veterinary, and safety standards. The UK government has been considering more stringent restrictions or a full ban due to concerns about animal welfare and public risk.

Across Europe, regulations are even stricter in many countries. For instance:

Germany allows squirrel monkey ownership under regulated conditions, with emphasis on space, enrichment, and social housing.

France requires licensing and compliance with national animal welfare laws.

Austria, Belgium, and Sweden generally ban the keeping of primates as pets altogether.

In Australia, it is illegal to keep squirrel monkeys as pets in all states and territories. The country's strict biosecurity laws prevent the importation and ownership of most non-native species to protect native wildlife and ecosystems.

In South American countries, where squirrel monkeys are indigenous, laws are focused more on conservation than private ownership. Countries like Brazil, Peru, and Colombia prohibit the capture and trade of wild primates and have banned or heavily restricted keeping them as pets. Illegal trafficking remains an issue, but national wildlife authorities increasingly crack down on offenders and rescue illegally kept primates.

Globally, CITES (the Convention on International Trade in Endangered Species of Wild Fauna and Flora) plays an important role. All squirrel monkeys are listed under Appendix II, which means international trade is regulated. Exporting or importing squirrel monkeys requires proper documentation and justification. This helps prevent illegal trafficking but does not necessarily affect domestic pet ownership laws.

Permits and Licensing

Where squirrel monkey ownership is legal or conditionally permitted, acquiring the right licenses and permits is a non-negotiable requirement. These legal documents are designed to ensure that the welfare of the animal is prioritized and that the owner is capable of meeting its needs. The requirements for obtaining a permit can be extensive and are often subject to regular review and renewal.

Typically, applicants must demonstrate the following:

Adequate housing: The enclosure must meet size and safety standards and provide enrichment and climate control.

Veterinary access: Owners must prove access to a licensed veterinarian with primate experience.

Zoning compliance: Some areas prohibit exotic animals in residential zones regardless of state or provincial legality.

Experience and training: Some jurisdictions require evidence of prior experience or training in handling primates or exotic animals.

Public safety precautions: There must be no reasonable threat to neighbors, children, or the public.

Once issued, licenses are often subject to surprise inspections by local authorities or wildlife officials. Non-compliance may result in fines, confiscation of the animal, or revocation of the license.

Moreover, licensing is not permanent. Permits often need to be renewed annually, with updated documentation and inspection results. The bureaucratic process can be time-consuming and costly, adding another layer of commitment to ownership.

Ethics of Keeping Primates as Pets

Beyond the legal landscape lies a deeper, more complicated question: Should squirrel monkeys be kept as pets at all? The ethical concerns surrounding primate ownership go well beyond legality. They encompass animal welfare, psychological well-being, conservation implications, and the broader societal message sent by domesticating wild species.

Squirrel monkeys are not domesticated animals. Unlike dogs or cats, they have not evolved alongside humans to form mutually beneficial relationships. Their instincts, needs, and behaviors are rooted in millions of years of evolution in the wild. Attempting to mold them into household pets often leads to emotional distress, behavioral issues, and suffering.

One of the greatest ethical concerns is social deprivation. Squirrel monkeys are naturally group-living creatures that depend on complex social interaction for emotional and psychological health. In the wild, they live in multi-individual troops where grooming, play, conflict resolution, and communication are daily affairs. Keeping a monkey isolated or with limited interaction—even with humans—deprives it of the rich social life it needs to thrive.

Captive monkeys often develop abnormal behaviors such as pacing, self-biting, rocking, or repetitive motions—clear signs of psychological distress. These behaviors, known as stereotypies, are seen in animals unable to express their natural instincts. Even well-meaning owners may fail to provide the level of enrichment and stimulation squirrel monkeys require to avoid these outcomes.

There are also ethical questions about the source of pet monkeys. While some may be captive-bred by licensed breeders, others are torn from the wild or bred in inhumane conditions. Infant monkeys may be separated from their mothers too early to imprint on humans, which can cause long-term trauma. The exotic pet trade—legal and illegal—often prioritizes profit over welfare, resulting in poor husbandry practices and high mortality rates.

Additionally, keeping primates as pets perpetuates the commodification of wildlife. When squirrel monkeys are treated as novelty pets or status symbols, it undermines conservation education and encourages the mistaken belief that wild animals can be adequately cared for in domestic settings. This contributes to the ongoing cycle of demand that fuels poaching and illegal trade.

For many animal welfare organizations, the answer is clear: primates, including squirrel monkeys, belong in the wild or in accredited sanctuaries and zoological facilities, not in private homes. Their intelligence and sensitivity deserve more than captivity can typically offer.

Responsibilities of Exotic Pet Ownership

Despite the challenges and concerns, some people do choose to keep squirrel monkeys—legally and under tightly controlled conditions. For those individuals, the responsibilities are enormous and must be approached with seriousness and foresight.

Owning a squirrel monkey requires substantial time and financial commitment. These animals may live 20 years or more in captivity. During this time, they need daily social interaction, a diverse diet, a highly enriched living environment, and frequent veterinary care.

The cost of initial setup can be thousands of dollars. Housing must include space for climbing, swinging, hiding, and foraging. Heating, humidity control, UV lighting, and sanitation must all be carefully managed. Enrichment items such as puzzle feeders, ropes, platforms, and mirrors must be rotated regularly to prevent boredom.

Their dietary requirements go far beyond feeding fruits and vegetables. Squirrel monkeys need a specific balance of protein, fiber, vitamins, and minerals. They often require live insects or specialty primate chow, which may not be readily available in all areas.

Owners must also contend with behavioral challenges. Squirrel monkeys can be loud, messy, and unpredictable. They may bite, throw feces, or mark territory with urine. During mating season, males may become aggressive or difficult to handle. These behaviors are natural but often intolerable in a household setting.

Another critical responsibility is long-term planning. What happens if the owner falls ill, moves to a region where monkey ownership is banned, or simply can no longer care for the animal? Many sanctuaries are already overburdened and may not be able to accept surrendered monkeys. Rehoming a primate is far more complex than rehoming a dog or cat, often involving legal hurdles and transportation difficulties.

Finally, owners must be aware of public health risks. Squirrel monkeys can carry zoonotic diseases such as herpes B virus, hepatitis, and salmonella. Regular health checks, vaccinations, and proper hygiene are essential to protect both the monkey and the human caretakers.

Conclusion

The decision to keep a squirrel monkey as a pet is not one to be taken lightly. It exists at the intersection of law, ethics, and immense personal responsibility. While legal ownership is possible in some jurisdictions, it is heavily restricted and rightly so. These intelligent, social animals require far more than most households can provide.

From a moral standpoint, the captivity of squirrel monkeys raises serious concerns about welfare, psychological well-being, and the integrity of wild populations. The exotic pet trade remains rife with exploitation and misinformation, and individuals who genuinely care about animals must question whether possession is ever the right path.

Responsible exotic animal ownership—when permitted—demands total commitment, substantial resources, and a deep respect for the animal's nature. For many, the better alternative is to support conservation efforts, visit reputable sanctuaries, and advocate for the protection of squirrel monkeys in the wild—where they truly belong.

CHAPTER 5:

SOURCING AND ADOPTION

When it comes to bringing a squirrel monkey into one's home, the journey must begin with a critical and informed understanding of how to source the animal responsibly. This chapter explores the contrasts between ethical breeders and illegal wildlife trade, explains how to identify a healthy monkey, discusses the adoption process through rescues or sanctuaries, and delves into the financial considerations associated with purchasing, maintaining, and ethically caring for a squirrel monkey.

The Importance of Ethical Sourcing

Squirrel monkeys are intelligent, social, and highly active primates native to Central and South America.

Their small size and curious demeanor often tempt individuals into purchasing them without full awareness of the complexities involved. Sadly, this demand has fueled a persistent and harmful illegal wildlife trade that contributes to the suffering of animals and the decline of wild populations.

Ethical sourcing begins with understanding the difference between legitimate breeders and those who engage in unlawful or inhumane practices. Ethical breeders prioritize the health, socialization, and long-term well-being of the animals. They often keep detailed health records, provide clean and enriched environments, and ensure babies are not separated prematurely from their mothers. By contrast, illegal traders or backyard breeders often keep animals in poor conditions, forgo veterinary care, and prioritize profit over welfare.

When you source a squirrel monkey through unethical means—whether knowingly or unknowingly—you risk perpetuating a cruel cycle of exploitation. Many monkeys sold through illegal channels are taken from the wild at a young age, transported in horrific conditions, and suffer trauma, disease, or death. Even in cases where monkeys survive the journey, they may struggle to adapt to captivity due to lack of socialization or chronic stress. Supporting ethical sources, therefore, is not only a personal responsibility but also a moral obligation to preserve wildlife and reduce suffering.

Identifying a Healthy Squirrel Monkey

Whether adopting through a breeder or a sanctuary, knowing what constitutes a healthy squirrel monkey is critical. A healthy monkey is alert, active, and curious. Its eyes should be bright and clear without any discharge. The fur should be dense and clean, without bald patches or signs of parasites. Look for consistent weight appropriate for the monkey's age and size— neither emaciated nor obese.

A healthy monkey should also demonstrate normal behaviors for its species. This includes grooming, vocalizing, exploring, and engaging with other monkeys (if present). Signs of illness or distress include lethargy, aggression, trembling, refusal to eat, diarrhea, or obsessive behaviors like pacing or self-mutilation.

Requesting veterinary records is a must. A reputable breeder or rescue will be able to provide documentation of vaccinations, parasite control, and health screenings. Furthermore, they should offer guidance on diet, enclosure setup, and social needs. Any reluctance to share this information should raise red flags.

It's also essential to observe the monkey's interaction with humans and other animals. A young monkey that has been hand-reared may appear more social, but if improperly socialized, it might later display behavioral problems as it matures. Wild-caught monkeys are especially prone to long-term psychological issues. A monkey that avoids eye contact, clings excessively, or shows signs of trauma may require specialized care and rehabilitation.

Adoption from Rescues and Sanctuaries

Adoption through rescues or sanctuaries provides an ethical alternative to purchasing, particularly for those committed to helping a primate in need. These organizations rescue monkeys from neglect, abuse, or illegal trade and work toward rehabilitating them physically and emotionally.

Adopting from a rescue requires a more in-depth screening process. Reputable sanctuaries ensure potential adopters are fully prepared for the lifelong commitment involved in caring for a primate. This includes understanding dietary needs, behavioral challenges, legal obligations, and the monkey's individual history. Some rescues may only offer long-term fostering or permanent sanctuary options rather than full adoption, especially in regions where it is illegal or unethical to keep primates in private homes.

It's important to understand that adopted monkeys may come with baggage. Many have experienced trauma, and may have behavior problems that require expert care and a great deal of patience. However, offering a second chance to a rescued animal can be a deeply rewarding experience for experienced and dedicated caregivers.

Adoption fees vary widely depending on the organization and the monkey's health needs. While often more affordable than purchasing from a breeder, ongoing care costs must still be anticipated. Additionally, sanctuaries will typically require that your home environment is properly prepared to accommodate a monkey's unique needs.

The Cost of Ownership

Purchasing a squirrel monkey is a significant financial commitment, and ownership costs extend far beyond the initial price tag. A baby squirrel monkey from an ethical breeder may cost anywhere from \$5,000 to \$8,000 USD, depending on its species, lineage, and breeder reputation. However, this cost is just the beginning.

Initial setup involves acquiring a large and enriched enclosure, preferably one that allows both indoor and outdoor access. Enclosures must provide climbing structures, hammocks, hiding spots, and a constant rotation of enrichment items to prevent boredom. These setups can cost several thousand dollars to build properly. Smaller cages are wholly unsuitable and contribute to stress-related illnesses and behavioral issues.

Veterinary care is another substantial cost. Squirrel monkeys require exotic animal veterinarians familiar with primates, and these specialists can be hard to find and expensive. Routine wellness visits, vaccinations, fecal tests, and dental care add up quickly. Emergency care, including surgeries or treatment for injuries, can cost thousands of dollars. Some owners opt to purchase specialized pet insurance for exotics, which can offset some costs but may still come with high premiums.

Feeding a squirrel monkey a proper diet is also an ongoing expense. A well-rounded diet includes fresh fruits, vegetables, insects, commercial primate chow, and vitamin supplements. Because these monkeys have fast metabolism and high energy levels, their food must be provided multiple times a day and in rotation to maintain interest and nutritional balance.

Monkey-proofing your home or designated monkey area is another hidden cost. These animals are highly intelligent and curious, capable of opening drawers, dismantling toys, and accessing hazardous items if not properly secured. Pet owners must invest in childproof locks, escape-proof barriers, and constant supervision. Without these precautions, the risk of injury—to both monkeys and humans—is high.

Final Thoughts

The decision to source and adopt a squirrel monkey is not one to be taken lightly. These charismatic animals require lifelong commitment, specialized care, and a strong moral compass when it comes to sourcing. Supporting ethical breeders, choosing rescue options when available, and refusing to engage in the illegal trade of primates are all vital steps in protecting both individual animals and wild populations.

By choosing to adopt or buy responsibly, potential owners take the first step in becoming a part of a movement that values conservation, compassion, and long-term welfare. Squirrel monkeys deserve homes where they are respected, stimulated, and loved—not treated as novelties or status symbols.

Those who are not fully prepared for the responsibility and cost of ownership should consider supporting squirrel monkeys in other ways—such as symbolically adopting one through a sanctuary, volunteering time, or donating to organizations working to protect these animals in the wild. In the end, the well-being of the monkey should always come first, and that starts with how you choose to bring one into your life.

CHAPTER 6:

PREPARING YOUR HOME

Welcoming a squirrel monkey into your life is not a casual endeavor. These intelligent, social primates demand more than affection—they require a home environment that mimics the complexity of their native habitat. Preparing your home for a squirrel monkey involves addressing everything from physical space and mental stimulation to safety measures and structural modifications. In this chapter, we'll walk through how to set up your living environment to support the health, happiness, and longevity of a squirrel monkey under human care.

The Importance of Habitat Preparation

Squirrel monkeys (genus Saimiri) are highly active, agile creatures that spend much of their lives navigating the canopy of dense rainforests in Central and South America. Their natural behaviors include climbing, leaping, foraging, and interacting with troop members. Therefore, any captive setting must strive to meet their physical and psychological needs through ample space, enrichment, safety, and comfort. Failure to provide such conditions may lead to health problems, stress, or destructive behaviors like self-mutilation or aggression.

Indoor vs. Outdoor Enclosures

Indoor Environments

If you plan to house your squirrel monkey indoors, you need to transform an entire room (or a large portion of your home) into a primate-friendly space. A cage alone is insufficient; squirrel monkeys need continuous access to open spaces that allow for movement, exploration, and play. Indoor environments must be climate-controlled, secure, and adapted for climbing and swinging.

The space should have high ceilings if possible, to encourage vertical activity. Install secure climbing ropes, hanging platforms, ladders, and branches across the upper areas of the room. Walls should be monkey-proofed—this includes covering or removing anything sharp, breakable, or chewable. All electrical outlets must be sealed, and appliances should be kept out of reach.

Surfaces should be easy to clean, as squirrel monkeys can be messy. Tile or vinyl flooring is ideal. Ensure that the room is well-ventilated but free from drafts, and keep lighting on a natural circadian cycle that simulates day and night rhythms.

Outdoor Enclosures

Outdoor enclosures can offer enormous benefits, especially in climates that are similar to the monkey's tropical origins. An outdoor space provides access to fresh air, sunlight, and the ever-changing stimuli of nature. However, you must protect your monkey from predators, weather extremes, and potential escape routes.

A proper outdoor enclosure should be a large, fully enclosed aviary-style structure made from strong, rust-resistant wire mesh. The walls, floor, and ceiling must be secured to prevent climbing out or digging under. Roofing should provide protection from rain and intense sun, while the structure must be shaded and ventilated.

Inside, replicate a forest canopy as closely as possible using ropes, live or artificial plants, wooden perches, and hiding areas. Always include a temperature-controlled shelter where the monkey can retreat during cold or overly hot conditions. If your climate isn't suitable year-round, use the outdoor space as an enrichment area while keeping your monkey primarily indoors.

Space Requirements and Housing Design

Squirrel monkeys are small, but they are not low-maintenance pets. The minimum enclosure space should be at least 8 feet high, 10 feet wide, and 12 feet long for a single monkey, though bigger is always better. These monkeys thrive in vertical spaces and need to climb, leap, and swing regularly. Never rely solely on horizontal floor space.

Inside the enclosure or dedicated monkey room, consider designing multiple levels of activity zones. Each level can serve a different purpose: feeding, nesting, playing, and grooming. You can install platforms at varying heights, suspended bridges, rope tunnels, and hanging baskets. Allow freedom of movement between these zones, encouraging natural locomotion behaviors.

Incorporate hiding spots and shelters that provide security and rest. Soft bedding, blankets, and hammocks are popular options. Make sure all materials are washable and non-toxic. Visual barriers, such as curtains or partitions, help the monkey feel safe from perceived threats or overstimulation.

Additionally, water features like small fountains can offer stimulation and drinking opportunities, though they must be cleaned regularly to prevent contamination.

Enrichment, Furniture, and Climbing Structures

Mental and physical enrichment is non-negotiable when housing a squirrel monkey. In the wild, these primates engage in complex foraging, socializing, and problem-solving behaviors throughout the day. Captivity must replicate this engagement through interactive structures and constantly rotating enrichment tools.

Climbing Structures
Use a combination of ropes, vines, and ladders at different heights to encourage climbing. These should be securely anchored to walls or ceilings. Wooden beams and live branches offer additional grip and variety. Avoid plastic ropes or items that may become slippery or break under weight.

Hanging Furniture and Platforms

Install hammocks, tire swings, and hanging baskets to mimic natural resting and lookout points. Use sisal or natural-fiber materials when possible. Ensure that everything is properly secured and can support rapid movement and jumping.

Foraging Toys and Food Puzzles
Squirrel monkeys are natural foragers. Use puzzle feeders, treat balls, or homemade devices like paper rolls filled with fruit to engage their minds and mimic natural feeding patterns. Change the location and contents of these toys frequently to avoid habituation.

Visual and Auditory Enrichment
Mirrors, picture books, and safe objects with moving parts or bright colors can be intriguing. Some owners find that TVs or radios playing nature sounds can calm or interest their monkeys. However, it's essential to monitor how the monkey responds—some stimuli can be overstimulating.

Social Enrichment

If keeping a single monkey, human interaction must be frequent and engaging. Socially isolated monkeys can suffer severe psychological stress. Ideally, squirrel monkeys should be housed with companions, provided all animals are healthy, bonded, and compatible.

Monkey-Proofing Your Home

Whether your monkey has free reign of a room or entire sections of your home, monkey-proofing is essential for both the monkey's safety and the preservation of your living space. Squirrel monkeys are curious, mischievous, and clever escape artists. They explore using their hands and mouths and will chew, tug, or rip anything they find.

Remove or Seal Hazardous Items
Electrical cords, outlets, batteries, small objects, and chemicals must be completely inaccessible. Monkeys can chew wires or ingest toxic materials in an instant. Cover outlets with tamper-proof protectors, and store all cleaning agents, medicines, and sharp tools in locked cabinets.

Windows and Doors

Windows should be secured with bars or mesh. Screens are not sufficient—squirrel monkeys can tear through them. Doors must lock or have monkey-proof handles, as these primates can learn to open standard doorknobs over time.

Avoid Breakables

Remove anything breakable or valuable from the monkey's range. Glass objects, ceramics, or electronics should be kept in secured storage. Decorations like plants or picture frames may be attractive to your monkey but can quickly become projectiles or choking hazards.

Bathroom and Kitchen Hazards

Never leave a monkey unattended in rooms with water access. Sinks, bathtubs, and toilets can pose drowning risks. Kitchen equipment—like knives, blenders, or stoves—are extremely dangerous, and the kitchen should be off-limits unless tightly controlled.

Secure Trash and Food Items

Garbage cans must be locked or kept behind closed doors. Squirrel monkeys are opportunistic scavengers and will dig through trash or steal food left on counters. Ensure all food items are stored securely and that feeding follows a scheduled routine to discourage foraging in forbidden areas.

The Psychological Importance of a Thoughtful Setup

Creating an appropriate environment isn't just about preventing accidents—it's about nurturing a psychologically healthy animal. Squirrel monkeys under stress or boredom may exhibit neurotic behaviors such as pacing, rocking, or excessive grooming. These signs indicate a lack of stimulation or social interaction and must be addressed by reworking the environment or increasing attention.

A stimulating enclosure that changes regularly—through rearranged furniture, new enrichment items, or social interactions—can help mimic the unpredictability and excitement of a natural habitat. Rotating toys, adding natural branches, hiding new smells, or offering puzzle feeders can make a world of difference to a captive monkey's wellbeing.

Final Thoughts

Preparing your home for a squirrel monkey is not a one-time task—it's an ongoing commitment. These primates are intelligent, active, and emotionally complex animals that need a living space tailored to their instincts. You must design an environment that provides climbing opportunities, psychological stimulation, safety, and social interaction. Both indoor and outdoor setups require constant evaluation, adjustment, and enrichment. When done right, this preparation ensures your squirrel monkey thrives—not merely survives—in your care.

CHAPTER 7:

DIET AND NUTRITION

Understanding the proper dietary needs of squirrel monkeys is one of the most important aspects of providing responsible care. Their diet in the wild is incredibly diverse, and failing to replicate that variety in captivity can lead to health issues, behavioral problems, and a lower quality of life. In this chapter, we will explore the key principles of feeding squirrel monkeys, highlight the importance of a species-appropriate diet, and provide guidance on feeding schedules, nutritional supplements, and foods to avoid.

Natural Diet vs. Captive Feeding

In the wild, squirrel monkeys are omnivorous foragers with a strong inclination towards frugivory and insectivory. They consume a diet composed primarily of fruits, insects, small vertebrates, flowers, nectar, and various plant materials. Their feeding behavior is opportunistic, and they rely heavily on seasonally available resources in their native rainforest habitats. Because they are constantly on the move, squirrel monkeys often forage in large groups, communicating as they navigate tree canopies in search of food.

In captivity, recreating this diverse and ever-changing diet is not always practical, but it is essential to approximate it as closely as possible. The goal should be to provide a nutritionally complete and stimulating feeding routine that mirrors their wild dietary patterns in both nutritional content and variety. A balanced captive diet must include fresh fruits and vegetables, a reliable source of protein, enrichment foods such as insects, and commercial primate biscuits or pellets formulated specifically for small New World monkeys.

Squirrel monkeys are susceptible to nutritional deficiencies, particularly in captivity where diets are sometimes too limited or overly reliant on processed foods. Therefore, offering a wide range of fresh and wholesome ingredients is vital to maintaining optimal health.

Recommended Foods and Supplements

A healthy squirrel monkey diet in captivity should ideally consist of the following components:

1. Fruits and Vegetables

These should make up a significant portion of the monkey's daily diet, especially as a source of vitamins, fiber, and hydration. Recommended fruits include:

Bananas (in moderation due to sugar content)
Apples (seedless)
Papayas

Mangoes

Blueberries

Grapes (seedless)

Pears

Watermelon

Cantaloupe

Recommended vegetables include:

Sweet potatoes (cooked or steamed)

Carrots

Bell peppers

Zucchini

Kale

Spinach (in small amounts due to oxalates)

Cucumber

Broccoli (cooked to reduce gas)

Fruits should be fresh, ripe, and thoroughly washed. While fruits are naturally appealing to squirrel monkeys, they should be given in moderation due to high sugar content, which can lead to obesity and diabetes if not balanced with other food sources.

2. *Proteins*

Protein is essential, especially for young, growing monkeys and pregnant females. In the wild, squirrel monkeys consume various insects and small animals. In captivity, suitable protein sources include:

Hard-boiled eggs
Mealworms
Crickets
Waxworms (as a treat due to high fat)
Cooked chicken (unseasoned and skinless)
Tofu or boiled lentils (occasionally)

Live insects also offer mental stimulation and encourage natural foraging behavior.

3. *Commercial Primate Diets*

There are commercial primate chow products designed specifically for New World monkeys such as the squirrel monkey. These are typically fortified with essential vitamins and minerals to support overall health. Brands like Mazuri and Zupreem offer such options. While not a replacement for fresh food, these pellets should be offered daily as a dietary base.

4. Supplements

Due to the limitations of captive diets, supplements may be necessary. Commonly used dietary supplements include:

Vitamin D3 – New World monkeys are particularly prone to D3 deficiency, which can result in metabolic bone disease. If your monkey has limited sunlight exposure, supplementation or UVB lighting may be required.

Calcium – A calcium supplement may be needed to prevent bone issues, especially in growing or breeding monkeys.

Multivitamin powders – These can be lightly sprinkled on food (in correct dosage) to ensure nutritional completeness.

It's important to consult a veterinarian experienced in primate care before starting any supplement regimen, as incorrect dosing can be harmful.

Feeding Schedule and Portion Sizes

Squirrel monkeys should be fed multiple times throughout the day to mimic their natural foraging behavior. Ideally, they should receive three meals per day, along with a few snack-sized enrichments to keep them mentally engaged.

Sample Daily Feeding Routine:

Morning (8:00 AM – 9:00 AM): A portion of fresh fruit and vegetables with commercial primate chow and a small protein source such as a boiled egg or insects.

Midday (12:00 PM – 1:00 PM): A lighter fruit or vegetable snack and opportunity to forage for insects hidden in enrichment toys.

Evening (5:00 PM – 6:00 PM): A more substantial meal with vegetables, protein, and primate pellets, with supplements if needed.

Portion sizes depend on the age, weight, and activity level of the monkey. Generally, a healthy adult squirrel monkey will consume around 20% of its body weight in food per day. Observation and veterinary guidance are important to prevent overfeeding or underfeeding.

Feeding should not be restricted to bowls. Scatter-feeding, using puzzle feeders, and hiding food throughout their enclosure are all effective ways to encourage natural behaviors and prevent boredom.

Toxic and Harmful Foods to Avoid

Some foods are dangerous or even lethal to squirrel monkeys and must be avoided entirely. These include:

Avocado: Contains persin, which is toxic to many animals including monkeys.

Chocolate: Contains theobromine and caffeine, which can be fatal.

Caffeine (coffee, tea, soda): Highly toxic and should never be offered.

Alcohol: Even small amounts can be deadly.

Onions and garlic: Can cause gastrointestinal distress and damage red blood cells.

Rhubarb: Contains oxalates that can affect kidney function.

Raw legumes (like kidney beans): Contain lectins which are harmful when uncooked.

Fruit seeds and pits (apple seeds, peach pits, etc.): Contain cyanogenic compounds and pose a choking hazard.

Additionally, processed human foods such as chips, candy, fried foods, and anything containing artificial sweeteners like xylitol must be strictly avoided. These items provide no nutritional value and can lead to a host of metabolic disorders.

All foods should be fresh, properly washed, and cut into manageable pieces to prevent choking. Uneaten fresh food should be removed after a few hours to prevent spoilage and contamination.

Hydration

Fresh, clean water must be available at all times. Water bottles or shallow bowls can be used, but bottles are often preferred as they are less prone to contamination. Bowls should be weighted or secured to prevent spillage.

Some keepers offer diluted fruit juices as an occasional treat, but this should be rare due to sugar content. Never offer sodas or sugary drinks, as they contribute to weight gain and dental issues.

Special Dietary Needs by Life Stage

Infants: Require formula specifically designed for primates or orphaned exotic mammals. Cow's milk is unsuitable. As they grow, soft fruits and mashed foods are gradually introduced.

Juveniles: Have higher energy requirements and need regular feeding with a good balance of protein and carbohydrates.

Pregnant/Lactating Females: Require increased calcium and protein, along with access to high-quality, nutrient-dense foods.

Elderly Monkeys: May need softer foods due to dental issues and adjustments in caloric intake to prevent weight gain.

Conclusion

Feeding a squirrel monkey correctly is a daily commitment that requires thought, planning, and observation. A balanced and varied diet supports their physical health and mental wellbeing while replicating the diverse foraging experience they would encounter in the wild. Owners must be vigilant about both what to include and what to avoid, consulting regularly with exotic animal veterinarians to fine-tune the dietary plan for their individual monkey.

Offering a diet rich in fruits, vegetables, proteins, and supplemented by commercial primate foods and vital nutrients ensures a long, healthy, and fulfilling life in captivity. More than just nourishment, feeding time is also an opportunity for enrichment, bonding, and promoting natural behaviors in these intelligent and social animals.

CHAPTER 8:

DAILY CARE AND ENRICHMENT

Caring for a squirrel monkey (genus Saimiri) goes far beyond simply providing food and shelter. These are highly intelligent, active, and social primates with specific needs for stimulation, cleanliness, and interaction. Meeting their daily care and enrichment requirements is not just a matter of routine—it's a commitment to supporting their mental, emotional, and physical health. In this chapter, we delve into the essentials of daily care, hygiene, mental stimulation, enrichment strategies, and preventative measures against stress and boredom.

Grooming and Hygiene

Unlike some other primates, squirrel monkeys do not spend a large portion of their day grooming each other. In the wild, they do groom socially to reinforce bonds within their group, but not extensively. However, hygiene in captivity is still of utmost importance to prevent illness and promote comfort.

Bathing and Self-Cleaning: Squirrel monkeys are not animals that require or enjoy being bathed. They typically groom themselves and each other when in bonded pairs or groups. However, if your monkey gets into something messy or sticky, a quick wipe with a damp, warm cloth may suffice. Using baby wipes that are fragrance-free and alcohol-free can be a gentle alternative. Never submerge them in water or use soap or shampoo designed for humans.

Cage and Enclosure Cleaning: One of the biggest responsibilities in squirrel monkey care is maintaining a clean habitat. These monkeys are known to defecate frequently, often while moving or jumping, which means their enclosures can get dirty quickly. Daily spot-cleaning of feces and uneaten food is essential, along with weekly deep cleaning involving sanitizing floors, walls, ropes, and any toys.

Use pet-safe disinfectants and always rinse thoroughly. Bedding, if used, should be changed frequently. Floors should be non-porous and easy to wash. Proper ventilation is also critical to prevent odor buildup and mold formation.

Personal Hygiene of the Monkey: Most squirrel monkeys do a good job of keeping themselves clean. However, periodic health checks are crucial. This includes checking their fur for mats, wounds, parasites, or skin conditions. Their nails may need occasional trimming if they are not worn down naturally through climbing and playing. Always seek a trained exotic animal veterinarian for assistance in grooming tasks.

Creating Stimulating Environments

Squirrel monkeys are energetic and agile creatures that thrive in stimulating, ever-changing environments. A monotonous setting can quickly lead to boredom, frustration, and even depression. Therefore, creating a dynamic enclosure filled with opportunities for play, exploration, and mental engagement is vital.

Physical Environment Design: The enclosure should be multi-dimensional, allowing for vertical movement and leaping. Branches, ropes, and platforms should crisscross the space, encouraging natural behaviors like jumping, running, and climbing. Mimicking forest canopy layers in the design helps to replicate their wild behavior.

Incorporate different textures such as rope, wood, rubber, and soft materials to encourage tactile exploration. Rearranging elements in the enclosure periodically can offer new challenges and reduce habituation. Hidden compartments and changing layouts encourage exploration and problem-solving.

Social Enrichment: In the wild, squirrel monkeys live in large, complex groups with intricate social dynamics. While it's not always feasible to keep multiple monkeys, social enrichment should never be neglected. Human interaction, bonding time, vocal engagement, and even supervised interaction with other primates (where legal and safe) are crucial.

If keeping more than one monkey, ensure compatibility by observing their behavior closely. A socially enriched environment often leads to healthier, more content individuals.

Toys, Puzzles, and Training Exercises

Play and exploration are not just pastimes for squirrel monkeys—they are essential for their cognitive development and emotional health. Just as humans require intellectual stimulation, squirrel monkeys must be challenged to keep their minds sharp and spirits high.

Toys and Enrichment Objects: A wide variety of toys should be provided, rotated weekly to maintain novelty. Popular enrichment items include:

Puzzle feeders that require manipulation to access treats
Hanging balls and chewable items
Mirrors and reflective surfaces (though they may become territorial)
Plastic keys, stacking cups, and baby toys
Foraging trays filled with safe natural materials like hay, coconut husk, or shredded paper with treats hidden inside

Avoid toys with small parts that can be ingested or toxic materials. Toys must be durable and easy to clean.

Problem-Solving Puzzles: Puzzle toys designed for parrots or raccoons often work well for squirrel monkeys. These can include sliding drawers, twist-and-open devices, or toys that dispense food only after a sequence of actions.

Training for Stimulation: Positive reinforcement training is a powerful tool not only for behavior shaping but also for mental enrichment. Simple commands like "come," "touch," or "give" can be taught using clicker training or treat rewards. Advanced tasks, like identifying colors, opening locks, or mimicking actions, can offer high levels of cognitive challenge.

This form of engagement strengthens the bond between the monkey and caretaker, enhances communication, and allows for easier handling and medical checkups.

Preventing Boredom and Stress

Boredom is a serious problem in captive primates, and squirrel monkeys are no exception. These animals have complex brains and social needs, and when these are unmet, they can develop abnormal behaviors such as pacing, fur plucking, rocking, or aggression.

Variety and Rotation: Changing the environment regularly is key. Rotating toys and perches, rearranging climbing structures, and introducing new scents or objects can dramatically reduce monotony. You can use spices, herbs, or even non-toxic flower petals to introduce new smells and tastes.

Sensory Enrichment: Squirrel monkeys are highly visual and auditory creatures. Playing sounds of rainforest environments, monkey vocalizations, or calming instrumental music can enrich their sensory world. Watching videos of animals, especially other monkeys, may intrigue them and simulate social observation.

Food-Based Enrichment: Scatter-feeding and hiding food in different areas or objects can replicate the effort and strategy required to forage in the wild. Frozen fruit treats, foraging boards, and stuffed cardboard rolls all encourage natural feeding behaviors.

Time With Caretakers: A strong human-monkey bond is central to the monkey's psychological well-being, especially for singly housed individuals. Spending time talking, playing, or even just being in their presence while reading or working can meet their social needs. Physical touch, if the monkey enjoys it, such as scratching or holding, should be consistent and respectful of the animal's comfort.

Avoiding Overstimulation: While stimulation is important, it's equally essential not to overwhelm them. Loud noises, too many new things at once, or constant changes can cause stress. Allowing periods of rest and retreat is critical, which is why quiet corners, hiding spots, and elevated resting areas should be built into the enclosure.

Monitoring Health Through Behavior

Daily care isn't just about providing resources—it's about observing. A caretaker should take time each day to watch for changes in energy, posture, appetite, and interactions. A healthy, enriched monkey is active, curious, social, and alert. A monkey showing signs of excessive sleepiness, withdrawal, aggression, or repetitive behaviors might be under-stimulated or unwell.

Even subtle changes, like chewing on enclosure bars or hiding more frequently, could indicate mental distress. Preventing boredom and stress isn't a one-time act—it's a dynamic process of adjusting care as the monkey grows and changes.

Conclusion

Squirrel monkeys, with their boundless energy, clever minds, and social complexity, require far more than just a clean cage and three meals a day. Their daily care must address not only their physical hygiene but their emotional and cognitive well-being. By providing varied, enriching environments and engaging them with meaningful interactions and tasks, you can ensure your monkey remains healthy, happy, and mentally stimulated.

Neglecting these needs can lead to profound suffering. But with commitment, creativity, and empathy, caregivers can offer squirrel monkeys a life that, while not identical to the wild, honors their nature and fulfills their needs.

CHAPTER 9:

HEALTH AND VETERINARY CARE

Squirrel monkeys, like all primates, require specialized care to ensure a long, healthy, and enriching life in captivity. Their small size and delicate systems mean that even minor illnesses or environmental stresses can quickly escalate into serious medical concerns. Understanding their unique health needs, recognizing early warning signs, establishing a preventive care routine, and partnering with a primate-experienced veterinarian are all critical aspects of responsible ownership.

Common Health Issues in Squirrel Monkeys

Despite their active and agile nature, squirrel monkeys are vulnerable to several health conditions that are either common in the species or arise due to captive care practices. Some health issues are preventable through appropriate housing, diet, and hygiene, while others are inherent biological vulnerabilities.

1. Nutritional Deficiencies: One of the most common problems seen in captive squirrel monkeys stems from improper diet. A diet that lacks essential nutrients—particularly vitamin D3, calcium, and vitamin C—can lead to metabolic bone disease, scurvy, and neurological symptoms. Monkeys that do not receive adequate UVB lighting or dietary supplements may also develop rickets or osteomalacia, both of which weaken the skeletal system.

2. Gastrointestinal Disorders: Diarrhea, constipation, and vomiting are frequently reported among pet squirrel monkeys. These symptoms can be caused by dietary imbalances, bacterial infections, intestinal parasites, or the ingestion of contaminated food or foreign objects. Gastrointestinal distress can lead to dehydration and rapid decline in small primates.

3. Respiratory Infections: Due to their sensitive lungs, squirrel monkeys are susceptible to respiratory conditions such as bronchitis, pneumonia, and upper respiratory infections. These can be caused by drafts, exposure to cigarette smoke, poor ventilation, or zoonotic pathogens passed from humans to primates.

4. Skin Conditions and Parasites: Mites, lice, fleas, and fungal infections can all affect squirrel monkeys, especially those kept in environments that are not properly sanitized. Excessive grooming, hair loss, scabbing, and skin irritation are red flags for ectoparasites or dermatological issues.

5. Trauma and Injuries: Due to their playful and energetic nature, squirrel monkeys can accidentally injure themselves. Falls, entanglements, burns, or cuts from unsafe enclosures or furnishings are not uncommon. Owners must monitor the safety of the monkey's environment closely and be prepared to respond to injuries quickly.

6. *Dental Problems:* Dental diseases like gingivitis, tooth decay, or broken teeth often result from an improper diet that lacks chewing variety or includes too much sugar. Routine oral inspections and offering natural, hard-textured foods help in maintaining oral hygiene.

7. *Psychological Disorders:* Captive squirrel monkeys may develop mental health issues such as anxiety, depression, or stereotypic behaviors (like pacing or self-harm) if they are under-stimulated, isolated, or improperly socialized. These behavioral health problems are as serious as physical illnesses and should never be ignored.

Recognizing Signs of Illness and Injury

The earlier an illness or injury is detected, the higher the chances of successful treatment and recovery. Squirrel monkeys, however, are masters at hiding their symptoms due to natural instincts that prevent predators from targeting the weak. Therefore, caregivers must be extremely observant of behavioral and physical changes.

Some of the most critical signs to watch for include:

Changes in Appetite or Water Intake: Refusal to eat, reduced appetite, or excessive drinking can signal internal issues, including gastrointestinal or kidney problems.

Altered Behavior or Lethargy: A normally active and curious monkey that suddenly becomes sluggish, irritable, or withdrawn may be suffering from illness or pain.

Unusual Vocalizations or Silence: A marked increase in vocalizations—especially distress calls—or sudden quietness can be signs of stress, pain, or disorientation.

Weight Loss or Obesity: Regular weighing is essential. Unexplained weight loss or weight gain may signal metabolic imbalances or improper diet.

Runny Nose, Sneezing, or Coughing: Respiratory signs should be taken seriously, especially if accompanied by lethargy, labored breathing, or nasal discharge.

Unkempt Coat or Hair Loss: Dull fur, bald patches, or excessive scratching may point to malnutrition, stress, parasites, or skin infections.

Discharge from Eyes or Genitals: Discharge is often a sign of infection or inflammation and should prompt immediate veterinary evaluation.

Abnormal Stool or Urine: Diarrhea, constipation, bloody stool, or urine with an unusual smell or color can indicate infections or dietary issues.

Limping or Reluctance to Move: These signs may indicate trauma, arthritis, or nerve issues and require diagnostic imaging.

Frequent observation of your monkey's behavior, eating habits, stool, and physical condition can help detect early signs of distress. A journal or logbook is useful for tracking patterns and sharing information with a vet when needed.

Preventative Care: Vaccinations, Parasite Control, and Hygiene

Preventative healthcare is one of the most vital components of primate ownership. It reduces the risk of disease outbreaks, ensures early diagnosis, and keeps the monkey comfortable and thriving.

Vaccinations: While not all countries have standardized vaccination schedules for squirrel monkeys, rabies, tetanus, and measles vaccines are often recommended or required in areas where these diseases are endemic.

Some facilities also administer vaccines for hepatitis and tuberculosis, especially when monkeys live in proximity to humans or other animals.

Parasite Control: Routine fecal examinations by a veterinarian help identify internal parasites such as roundworms or protozoa. External parasites like mites or lice can be managed through topical treatments and environmental sanitation. Preventive deworming and flea control should be scheduled at regular intervals, based on veterinary advice.

Sanitation: The monkey's enclosure, feeding dishes, toys, and bedding should be cleaned daily. Deep cleaning using animal-safe disinfectants should occur weekly to prevent bacterial and fungal buildup. Waste should be removed promptly, and any leftover food or spilled water must not be left to decay.

Dental and Nail Care: Monkeys naturally wear down their nails and teeth with climbing and chewing, but captive environments may not always facilitate this.

Offering gnawing materials and inspecting their oral and nail health regularly helps maintain comfort and function.

Routine Health Checks: Schedule a full health exam at least once or twice a year, depending on the monkey's age and medical history. These checkups may include bloodwork, dental inspection, imaging (X-ray or ultrasound), and physical examination.

Environmental Monitoring: Squirrel monkeys are sensitive to drafts, temperature changes, and high humidity. Installing thermometers and humidity gauges in the enclosure, providing UVB lighting, and ensuring good airflow without cold drafts are all part of maintaining a safe, health-supportive environment.

Finding a Primate-Savvy Veterinarian

One of the biggest challenges in squirrel monkey ownership is locating a veterinarian with experience in primate medicine. Not all vets are equipped to treat exotic animals, and primates—being so biologically close to humans—require very specific diagnostic and treatment protocols.

To find a suitable veterinarian:

1. Look for Exotic Animal Clinics: Some veterinary clinics specialize in exotic pets or zoo animals. These facilities are often more familiar with the anatomy, diseases, and behavioral issues of monkeys.

2. Ask for Referrals: Reach out to local wildlife centers, animal sanctuaries, or zoos. They may be able to recommend a trusted primate vet in your area.

3. Verify Experience: Before committing to a vet, ask questions about their training, experience with nonhuman primates, access to specialized equipment, and willingness to consult with veterinary colleges or specialists if needed.

4. Emergency Preparedness: Inquire whether the vet offers emergency care or if they can refer you to a 24-hour emergency hospital familiar with exotic species.

5. Build a Relationship: Establishing a long-term relationship with a veterinarian helps your monkey receive consistent care and allows the vet to become familiar with your pet's baseline health data, which is invaluable during times of illness.

Conclusion

Squirrel monkeys are incredibly intelligent, sensitive, and socially complex animals. Their health care needs are just as sophisticated. Understanding the types of health issues they face, observing closely for signs of distress, committing to a robust preventative care routine, and securing the services of a qualified primate veterinarian are all critical pillars of responsible ownership.

Maintaining a squirrel monkey in good health is not merely about treating illness when it arises—it is about creating an environment where disease is unlikely to occur, where the monkey's mental and physical needs are consistently met, and where early signs of trouble are not overlooked. With dedication, vigilance, and informed support, squirrel monkeys can thrive in captivity and offer their caregivers years of companionship and enrichment.

CHAPTER 10:

SOCIALIZATION AND BEHAVIOR MANAGEMENT

Squirrel monkeys (Saimiri spp.) are remarkably intelligent and social animals with complex behavioral repertoires. In the wild, they thrive in dynamic groups where social interaction plays a vital role in their survival, development, and well-being. When kept in captivity, especially as exotic pets, their behavioral and social needs do not diminish—in fact, they become even more important. Proper socialization and behavior management are essential for ensuring a squirrel monkey's health, emotional stability, and compatibility in a domestic setting.

This chapter will explore how to interpret squirrel monkey behavior, promote healthy bonding between monkey and human or among other primates, address behavioral problems, and use positive reinforcement training to support a balanced and enriched lifestyle for these complex creatures.

Understanding Natural Behaviors

Squirrel monkeys are among the most active and vocal primates in the animal kingdom. They are diurnal, arboreal creatures with an almost ceaseless curiosity and a need for constant stimulation. In the wild, they live in large multi-male, multi-female groups that can number between 20 and 75 individuals. Their survival strategy hinges on cooperation, communication, and alertness to predators and environmental changes.

Understanding their natural behaviors is crucial to interpreting their body language, vocalizations, and emotional state in captivity. Behaviors such as tail coiling, lip-smacking, vocal chattering, and piloerection (fur standing on end) all communicate specific messages within a troop. In captivity, these same behaviors can provide critical insights into the monkey's comfort, anxiety, happiness, or aggression.

Key natural behaviors include:

Social grooming: An essential bonding activity in primate groups, used to strengthen social ties.

Foraging and exploration: A significant portion of their time in the wild is spent foraging, so this drive must be simulated in captivity.

Vocalization: They produce a variety of sounds, from whistles to chatters and squeals, each conveying different intentions such as alerting to danger or seeking attention.

Territorial and dominance behaviors: These can include displays such as chasing, mounting, or physical gestures to assert hierarchy.

By understanding what is "normal" behavior for a squirrel monkey, caretakers can better identify when something is wrong—such as signs of stress, illness, or psychological distress.

Social Bonding with Humans and/or Other Monkeys

Squirrel monkeys are not solitary animals. Isolation from social contact can lead to psychological disorders, self-harm, and abnormal behaviors such as excessive pacing, rocking, or overgrooming. In the wild, their social environment is rich, complex, and constantly engaging. Mimicking this in captivity is challenging but not impossible.

Bonding with Humans

When kept as exotic pets, squirrel monkeys often look to their human caregivers for companionship. However, this relationship must be built slowly and respectfully. Forced handling, sudden movements, or loud noises can provoke fear or aggression. Establishing trust is a gradual process that relies on consistency, patience, and sensitivity.

Some recommended methods for bonding include:

Consistency in routines: Feeding, cleaning, and interaction should happen at predictable times.

Respecting personal space: Especially early on, the monkey should initiate contact.

Offering enrichment during social time: Use toys, puzzles, or treats during interactions to create positive associations.

Reading body language: Retreating, displaying teeth, or emitting warning sounds are signs that the monkey feels threatened.

Notably, no matter how bonded a monkey becomes with a human, they are still a wild animal by nature. There are limits to their domestic adaptability, and inappropriate handling can lead to defensive behaviors.

Housing with Other Monkeys

Keeping more than one squirrel monkey is ideal in terms of mental stimulation and natural socialization. However, introducing monkeys to one another must be done with care. They have intricate social hierarchies, and a rushed introduction can result in aggression or serious injury.

A gradual approach might include:

Visual exposure first: Let them see each other through mesh or glass for a period before physical contact.

Short, supervised interactions: Initially limited and always under observation.

Neutral territory: Introductions should take place in areas where neither monkey has established dominance.

Equal access to resources: Food, toys, and sleeping areas must be abundant to prevent competition.

Compatibility will depend on sex, age, individual temperament, and whether one or both were hand-reared by humans. Same-sex pairs, especially females, tend to do better together than mixed-sex pairs unless breeding is intended and legal.

Aggression, Fear, and Behavioral Challenges

Like all primates, squirrel monkeys can display aggression, fear responses, and a range of other behavioral challenges—particularly if their needs are not being met. Aggressive or fearful behaviors can emerge from a lack of socialization, improper handling, boredom, or health problems.

Types of Behavioral Challenges

1. Aggression

Causes: Inadequate space, frustration, perceived threats, hormonal changes during puberty, or overstimulation.

Signs: Biting, chasing, lunging, vocal threats, or urine marking.

Management: Provide adequate enrichment, ensure ample space, avoid sudden changes, and consult a behavioral expert when needed.

2. Fear-based Behaviors

Causes: Harsh handling, loud noises, sudden environmental changes, or trauma.

Signs: Cowering, retreating, freezing, screaming, or excessive defecation.

Management: Gradual desensitization, quiet environments, and trust-building interactions.

3. Stereotypic Behaviors

Causes: Chronic stress or boredom.

Signs: Rocking, pacing, excessive grooming, or repetitive movements.

Management: Increase cognitive and environmental enrichment, social contact, and daily routine variation.

4. Resource Guarding

Causes: Competition for food, toys, or sleeping areas.

Signs: Aggression during feeding, hoarding, or blocking access.

Management: Provide multiple feeding stations and duplicate enrichment items.

5. Sexual Behaviors

Males, in particular, may exhibit seasonal increases in sexual aggression during breeding season. This is managed by separating individuals, neutering (if permitted and safe), or through behavioral redirection.

Behavioral challenges are not signs of a "bad" monkey, but of an unmet need. Owners must respond with empathy, structure, and strategies that reflect the monkey's natural behavior rather than punishment or isolation.

Positive Reinforcement Training Techniques

Training squirrel monkeys can significantly improve their quality of life in captivity. It can also reduce stress during veterinary visits, feeding, cleaning, and enrichment changes. Positive reinforcement—a method based on rewarding desired behavior rather than punishing undesired behavior—is the most humane and effective training method for primates.

Key principles of positive reinforcement training include:

Clear communication: Use consistent verbal cues or hand signals.

Timing is critical: Reinforcement must follow immediately after the correct behavior.

Motivating rewards: Use highly valued items such as pieces of fruit, insects, or access to favored toys.

Short sessions: Squirrel monkeys have short attention spans, so training sessions should be brief and fun.

Consistency: Everyone interacting with the monkey must use the same cues and rewards.

Basic training goals might include:

Target training: Teaching the monkey to touch a stick or object, helpful for guiding movement.

Recall training: Teaching the monkey to come when called.

Stationing: Teaching the monkey to stay on a perch or platform, useful for medical checks.

Desensitization: Getting the monkey comfortable with handling, tools, or veterinary procedures.

Training also serves as enrichment, challenging their brains and giving them a sense of control and accomplishment. Owners should avoid negative reinforcement, fear-based tactics, or isolation, which can lead to distrust and worsened behavior.

Managing Behavioral Changes Over Time

Squirrel monkeys undergo behavioral changes as they age. Juveniles are generally more curious, excitable, and energetic, while adults can be more territorial, assertive, and cautious. Hormonal changes, especially during puberty, can dramatically affect temperament and sociability.

Caretakers must be prepared for:

Shifts in dominance: Particularly if more than one monkey is housed together.
Emergence of mating behaviors: Males may become more aggressive during mating season.
Bonding shifts: As they mature, they may form preferences or distance from certain individuals.

Regular observation, consistent routines, ongoing enrichment, and attentive care will help manage these transitions. Consulting with primate behaviorists or veterinarians during key life stages is also advisable.

Conclusion

Squirrel monkeys are highly intelligent, socially intricate, and behaviorally demanding creatures. Proper socialization and behavior management are central to their well-being in captivity. Understanding their natural instincts, providing appropriate companionship, responding to behavioral challenges with compassion, and using positive reinforcement training are all critical components of responsible monkey ownership.

Their behaviors are not random or malicious but rooted in thousands of years of evolution. To respect them as sentient beings, caregivers must adapt their environments, expectations, and methods to meet the psychological and social needs of these fascinating primates. When given proper care, love, and respect, squirrel monkeys can form deeply enriching and complex relationships with both humans and other monkeys—highlighting just how special and misunderstood they truly are.

CHAPTER 11:

BREEDING AND REPRODUCTION (OPTIONAL CHAPTER FOR BREEDERS)

Breeding squirrel monkeys in captivity is an endeavor that requires profound commitment, comprehensive knowledge, and an ethical mindset. This chapter explores the reproductive biology and behavior of squirrel monkeys, outlines the process of breeding and raising young in a captive environment, and underscores the ethical and logistical concerns that must be weighed by anyone considering this responsibility. Although breeding may appeal to enthusiasts hoping to expand captive populations or contribute to conservation programs, it is not a casual task and must always be approached with care and accountability.

Breeding Age and Reproductive Cycles

Squirrel monkeys (genus Saimiri) reach sexual maturity at different ages depending on their sex and the specific species. Typically, males mature around 4 to 5 years of age, while females may become sexually mature by the age of 2.5 to 3 years. However, physical maturity does not always equate to behavioral readiness, and animals that are technically of breeding age may not yet exhibit the social stability or physical condition suitable for successful mating or rearing of offspring.

Squirrel monkeys exhibit a seasonal breeding cycle, heavily influenced by environmental factors like photoperiod, humidity, and food availability. In the wild, mating generally occurs in the dry season, followed by births at the beginning of the wet season when food is more plentiful. In captivity, this cycle may persist unless interrupted or altered by artificial lighting and stable food supplies. It's vital to monitor these cues and mimic natural rhythms if one wishes to support reproductive success while ensuring animal well-being.

Females have a menstrual cycle lasting approximately 7 to 10 days, and behavioral cues such as increased vocalization or genital swelling can indicate estrus. Close monitoring, however, is required to interpret these signs accurately.

Mating Behavior

Squirrel monkeys demonstrate intricate social and sexual behaviors, especially during the breeding season. Males undergo a phenomenon known as "fattening" or seasonal fatting, where they bulk up, particularly in the upper body and shoulders. This is not due to fat accumulation alone but also water retention and muscle growth, triggered by hormonal changes that signal breeding readiness. This visual transformation often correlates with heightened status among other males.

During mating, males court females with displays of grooming, body posturing, and scent marking. Copulation is brief and may be repeated frequently over several days. In multi-male groups, dominant males typically gain the majority of mating opportunities, though subordinate males may still occasionally breed if social tensions are low or if they form a special bond with a receptive female.

Breeders must take care to manage group dynamics carefully to avoid excessive aggression or injury. Placing breeding pairs or trios in isolated enclosures during the mating season is often advised to ensure successful mating and prevent stress or social conflict.

Pregnancy and Gestation

Once mating is successful, the female's gestation period will last around 150 to 170 days, depending on the species. During this time, physical changes will gradually become apparent. The abdomen will swell noticeably in the later stages, and the female may show changes in behavior, such as reduced activity, increased appetite, or a preference for solitude.

Throughout pregnancy, the female should be provided with enhanced nutrition, including extra protein, calcium, and vitamin-rich foods. Enrichment activities should be gentle and non-strenuous to avoid stress, while housing should be stable and comfortable. It is imperative to avoid disturbing the pregnant female unnecessarily, and all veterinary check-ups should be performed with minimal stress.

Monitoring the female for signs of complications such as lethargy, discharge, or prolonged restlessness is essential. In rare cases, veterinary intervention may be required for dystocia (difficulty in labor), but this is typically uncommon in healthy, well-managed animals.

Birth and Infant Care

Most squirrel monkey births occur during the early hours of the morning or at night when the environment is calm.

The female usually delivers a single infant, although twins are rare but possible. Birth is generally a quick and instinctual process, and mothers often care for their newborns without intervention.

Neonates are extremely small and fragile, typically weighing between 80 to 100 grams. They cling to their mother's back almost immediately after birth. For the first several weeks, the infant remains latched to the mother's body, nursing frequently and relying entirely on her for warmth, nutrition, and security.

Captive mothers should be monitored discreetly to ensure proper bonding and care. Excessive human interference may stress the mother or cause rejection. If a mother shows signs of neglecting the infant, is ill, or has died during birth, hand-rearing may be necessary—a labor-intensive and delicate process that requires specialized milk replacers, around-the-clock feeding, and careful hygiene.

As the infant grows, it begins to explore its environment under the mother's supervision, gradually reducing its dependency by 4 to 6 months. Weaning typically occurs around 6 to 8 months of age, but some individuals may nurse longer depending on the social group's structure and maternal instincts.

Socialization of Juveniles

Once weaned, juvenile squirrel monkeys benefit greatly from social interaction with others of their kind. Keeping them isolated from peers may lead to behavioral issues or social development delays. Young monkeys should be integrated into age-appropriate groups where they can learn communication, foraging, and play behavior.

Captive breeding facilities must have plans in place for housing, socializing, and long-term care of juvenile monkeys. It is unethical and irresponsible to breed without the resources and space to provide proper care for the resulting offspring.

Socialization with humans is not a substitute for same-species interaction, and the psychological well-being of juvenile monkeys is heavily dependent on their ability to form normal social bonds.

Ethical Concerns and Population Control

The topic of breeding squirrel monkeys raises serious ethical considerations, especially concerning overpopulation, welfare, and the impact on conservation efforts. With thousands of primates already in sanctuaries or unsuitable homes due to the exotic pet trade, breeders must act responsibly and ask themselves whether adding to the captive population is justified.

Breeding should never be pursued purely for profit or novelty. It should be reserved for:

Accredited breeding programs aiming to maintain genetic diversity.

Conservation-related efforts supporting endangered populations in legitimate, species-appropriate environments.

Scientific institutions adhering to strict ethical standards and welfare regulations.

Irresponsible or indiscriminate breeding can contribute to the illegal wildlife trade, oversaturation of animals needing care, and decline in animal welfare. If animals are being produced faster than they can be homed appropriately, serious moral questions arise.

To prevent such outcomes, ethical breeders should practice population control, which may involve selective breeding, sterilization of surplus individuals, or ceasing breeding altogether when demand or resources cannot justify it.

Additionally, all breeding practices must comply with local, regional, and international laws concerning exotic animal breeding, trade, and transport. This includes adherence to CITES (Convention on International Trade in Endangered Species), USDA regulations (for U.S. breeders), and welfare standards prescribed by animal health and conservation organizations.

Conclusion

Breeding squirrel monkeys is not a task to be undertaken lightly. While it can be rewarding when carried out ethically and responsibly, it demands high levels of care, knowledge, resources, and long-term planning. From understanding natural reproductive behaviors to managing the health and social needs of mothers and infants, breeders must prioritize animal welfare at every step.

In a world where many primates are threatened by habitat loss, poaching, and illegal trade, breeding should be driven not by curiosity or commerce but by a genuine commitment to the well-being of the species. Whether you're a prospective breeder or simply a dedicated monkey caretaker, the decision to breed squirrel monkeys must always be made with the highest ethical standards and a strong sense of stewardship.

CHAPTER 12:

LIFESPAN, AGING, AND END-OF-LIFE CARE

Squirrel monkeys (genus Saimiri) are among the most captivating and intelligent primates in the world. As exotic pets or members of zoological collections, they require diligent care throughout their lives. One of the most overlooked yet critically important aspects of primate ownership is planning for the long haul—including their lifespan, aging process, and end-of-life care. This chapter aims to equip you with a compassionate and realistic understanding of what to expect as your squirrel monkey ages, including how to support them medically, emotionally, and ethically until the very end.

Life Expectancy in Captivity

Squirrel monkeys typically live longer in captivity than in the wild due to the availability of food, veterinary care, and protection from predators and environmental hazards. In the wild, squirrel monkeys may only live between 12 to 15 years due to risks such as disease, predation, and environmental stress. In captivity, with excellent care, they can live well into their early to mid-20s, with some individuals reportedly reaching 25 years or more.

This extended lifespan is both a blessing and a responsibility. Prospective owners must be prepared for a two-decade commitment. During this time, a squirrel monkey will transition through various life stages—infancy, adolescence, adulthood, and senior years—each with unique physical, behavioral, and emotional needs.

Recognizing the Aging Process

Understanding the aging process in squirrel monkeys allows caregivers to detect early signs of decline and proactively support their animals. Aging is often gradual and may manifest differently depending on genetics, environment, and historical health care. Some of the most common signs of aging include:

Decreased mobility and agility: Older monkeys may move more slowly, become less agile in climbing, or prefer resting over play.

Graying fur: Just like humans, some squirrel monkeys show signs of gray or thinning hair, especially around the face.

Weight changes: Aging may lead to either weight gain due to decreased activity or weight loss due to metabolic changes or underlying illnesses.

Altered social behavior: Senior monkeys might withdraw from group interactions or become less interested in human interaction.

Cognitive decline: Some squirrel monkeys may display signs similar to cognitive dysfunction syndrome, such as forgetfulness, confusion, or repetitive behaviors.

Changes in sensory function: Decline in hearing or vision is common with age, and monkeys may startle more easily or misjudge distances.

Diminished appetite or altered dietary needs: They may become pickier eaters or require softer foods due to dental issues.

Recognizing these signs early helps ensure that proper accommodations and interventions can be made to enhance the monkey's quality of life.

Senior Monkey Care

As squirrel monkeys age, they will require increasingly specialized care to maintain comfort and health. Here are some important components of senior care:

Environmental Modifications

Older monkeys may benefit from adjustments to their living environment. Lower platforms, ramps instead of ropes, padded flooring, and extra heating can make a world of difference in ensuring comfort and safety. Reduced mobility increases the risk of falls, so the enclosure should be modified to be senior-friendly while still allowing mental and physical stimulation.

Diet Adjustments

A senior squirrel monkey may require a more tailored diet. They may struggle with hard fruits or nuts due to dental decay or gum sensitivity. Offering soft fruits, cooked vegetables, and primate-specific senior food formulas can help maintain nutritional balance. Supplements such as glucosamine, omega-3 fatty acids, and probiotics may support joint health and digestion, but always consult a vet before introducing new supplements.

Dental Health

Dental issues are prevalent in aging primates. Routine dental checks should be part of their health regimen. Bad breath, drooling, difficulty chewing, or avoiding food are red flags. Dental disease can lead to infections, systemic health issues, and nutritional deficiencies, making preventive care essential.

Medical Monitoring

Older monkeys are more prone to chronic conditions such as arthritis, kidney or liver disease, diabetes, heart issues, and tumors. Regular veterinary visits—ideally twice a year—can help monitor organ function and detect disease early. Blood work, ultrasounds, and other diagnostics become increasingly important in geriatric primates.

Emotional Support and Mental Enrichment

Aging doesn't just affect the body—it also impacts the mind and spirit. As primates, squirrel monkeys possess deep emotional intelligence and complex social needs, even in later life.

Companionship

If the monkey is kept with a bonded companion or in a small social group, those bonds remain crucial throughout their senior years. Separating aging monkeys from familiar companions can cause psychological stress. However, if a monkey becomes the last of its group, caregivers must step in more actively to provide emotional support through interaction, affection, and attention.

Cognitive Stimulation

Cognitive enrichment remains vital even as energy levels decrease. Puzzle feeders, novel objects, scent trails, and gentle games keep the aging brain engaged and help stave off cognitive decline. However, keep activities low-stress and avoid overwhelming the animal. Some monkeys may even enjoy passive enrichment such as watching videos, listening to soothing music, or observing their environment from a cozy perch.

Managing Chronic Illness

As monkey caretakers, you will likely face chronic conditions or progressive illnesses that require a long-term care strategy. This might involve administering medication, changing diets, modifying the environment, or adapting enrichment protocols.

For example, a squirrel monkey with arthritis may benefit from anti-inflammatory medication or heated perches. Those with kidney problems may require a specialized diet with reduced protein and phosphorus. A monkey showing signs of dementia may need a routine-based environment and minimal changes to prevent confusion and distress.

It's critical to work closely with a veterinarian experienced in primate care. A good vet will help you develop a comprehensive care plan, educate you on medication management, and regularly review the monkey's quality of life.

End-of-Life Care

One of the hardest aspects of caring for a squirrel monkey—or any beloved animal—is facing the end of life. While some monkeys may pass naturally due to age-related decline, others may suffer from progressive illness that warrants euthanasia to prevent suffering.

End-of-life care should focus on comfort, dignity, and compassion. Signs that a monkey may be nearing the end of life include:

  Lack of interest in food or water
  Extreme weakness or inability to move
  Difficulty breathing or signs of severe pain
  Incontinence or complete loss of bodily function
  Withdrawal from social interaction and enrichment

Pain management becomes a top priority. Palliative care, including pain relief and supportive measures, can improve quality of life during the final stages. When suffering overtakes quality of life, euthanasia may be the most humane option. This decision is profoundly difficult, but many owners find peace in knowing they prevented further pain for their beloved companion.

Always discuss options with your veterinarian, who can guide you through the process, help assess the animal's condition objectively, and support you in making the kindest decision possible.

Coping with Grief and Loss

Losing a squirrel monkey—especially one you've raised and loved for decades—is a deeply emotional experience. The bond between a human and a primate is unlike any other. These animals are highly intelligent, expressive, and social, forming meaningful relationships with their caregivers.

Grief is natural and may manifest as sadness, guilt, or even anger. Give yourself space to mourn. Share memories with others who understand, such as other exotic pet owners, online primate communities, or grief support groups. Creating a memorial, photo album, or planting a tree in their honor can offer comfort.

For some, the idea of adopting another monkey may arise. It's important to wait until you feel emotionally ready and are capable of starting the commitment all over again—ethically and responsibly.

Legacy of Care

Providing a high-quality life for a squirrel monkey from youth through old age is one of the most rewarding challenges in exotic pet ownership. Aging is not a decline in value or importance—it is a phase where your monkey relies on your experience, empathy, and dedication more than ever.

Your efforts during the senior years leave a lasting legacy of love and care. Whether your monkey was a rescue, a former lab subject, or a lifelong companion, your commitment gives them something that many primates never experience—comfort, dignity, and the gentle kindness of a devoted guardian.

CHAPTER 13:

SQUIRREL MONKEYS IN RESEARCH AND ENTERTAINMENT

Squirrel monkeys (genus Saimiri) are small, highly intelligent New World primates native to Central and South America. Their remarkable cognitive abilities, expressive faces, and sociable behavior have made them both subjects of scientific fascination and stars in entertainment. However, their use in laboratories and media has also sparked intense ethical debate. This chapter explores the historical and modern roles of squirrel monkeys in research and entertainment, examining how human fascination with these primates has led to exploitation, how public perception has evolved, and what responsibilities we now bear in safeguarding their welfare.

A History of Use in Scientific Research

Squirrel monkeys have played a significant role in biomedical research since the mid-20th century. Their small size, relative ease of care in controlled environments, and biological similarities to humans have made them valuable subjects in studies relating to neurology, behavior, pharmacology, and infectious diseases.

In the 1950s and 1960s, squirrel monkeys were heavily used in psychological experiments aimed at understanding learning and memory. Their quick learning abilities and capacity to interact with experimental apparatus like levers and touchscreens made them ideal subjects for operant conditioning studies. These experiments contributed to major discoveries in behavioral science and the development of theories still taught today.

Squirrel monkeys were also instrumental in space research during the space race. NASA and other agencies used them to test the effects of microgravity on biological organisms. Monkeys were launched into suborbital flights to observe physiological and behavioral responses to zero-gravity environments, providing foundational data for human spaceflight preparation.

Additionally, squirrel monkeys have been used extensively in drug testing and neurological research. Their brain structures bear notable similarities to those of humans, particularly in terms of the neocortex, making them useful in studying Alzheimer's disease, Parkinson's disease, and addiction. They have been used to observe the long-term effects of cocaine, nicotine, amphetamines, and opioids.

Despite the contributions to science, these research practices have not been without significant ethical concerns. The conditions in which research animals have been kept—often isolated, in small enclosures, and subject to painful or stressful procedures—have raised alarms among animal welfare advocates and the public.

Ethical Concerns and Shifting Perspectives

As public awareness of animal rights has grown, so too has the scrutiny of using primates, including squirrel monkeys, in research. The late 20th and early 21st centuries have seen a marked shift in how such practices are viewed.

One of the most significant concerns is the emotional and psychological impact on squirrel monkeys used in laboratories. These primates are highly social and require constant interaction, stimulation, and environmental enrichment. When kept in isolation or deprived of mental engagement, they can develop severe stress-related behaviors such as self-harming, repetitive pacing, and depression.

Animal advocacy organizations like PETA, the Humane Society, and Born Free USA have documented and exposed conditions in primate research facilities. Graphic footage and reports have catalyzed widespread condemnation, leading to reforms in animal testing regulations and the implementation of ethical review boards for research involving primates.

Many nations and institutions have begun phasing out or heavily regulating primate research. The European Union, for example, has implemented strict rules under Directive 2010/63/EU that limit the use of non-human primates in scientific procedures. In the United States, the National Institutes of Health (NIH) announced the end of chimpanzee research in 2015, and although squirrel monkeys are still used in some studies, the trend is toward reduction and refinement.

Ethical alternatives, such as computer simulations, organ-on-chip technology, and genetically modified rodents, are now increasingly preferred for research once performed on primates. In some cases, retired research monkeys are relocated to sanctuaries where they can live out the rest of their lives in more naturalistic conditions.

The Role of Squirrel Monkeys in Entertainment

Squirrel monkeys have also been popular in the entertainment industry, particularly throughout the 20th century. Their small size, expressive faces, and trainability made them appealing for films, television, circuses, and even roadside attractions.

Historically, squirrel monkeys were featured in vaudeville acts, carnivals, and traveling animal shows. Later, they appeared in TV shows and movies, often dressed in human-like costumes or performing tricks. Their cute and clever behavior made them popular with audiences and a staple of exotic animal performances.

For example, in movies and television, squirrel monkeys have been portrayed as sidekicks or comic relief characters. One of the most famous fictional representations is the character of "Jack the Monkey" in the Pirates of the Caribbean film series. Although a capuchin monkey played that specific role, squirrel monkeys were often used for similar comic and visually appealing roles.

In the 1960s and 70s, it was not uncommon to see squirrel monkeys kept as exotic pets by celebrities or exhibited in petting zoos. Some were even used in advertising, often dressed in clothing or used to attract attention in commercials.

Unfortunately, behind the scenes, many of these monkeys endured stressful and unnatural conditions. Forced training, rough handling, and inadequate housing led to high rates of stress and behavioral disorders. Some were declawed or had their teeth removed to make them "safer" to work with—practices now widely condemned.

Changing Views on Primates in Entertainment

Just as with scientific research, public attitudes toward using animals—especially intelligent primates like squirrel monkeys—for entertainment have dramatically shifted.

Documentaries such as Project Nim and The Life of Primates have highlighted the emotional and cognitive complexity of monkeys, increasing empathy and awareness. This has led to widespread campaigns against the use of primates in circuses and television, resulting in bans and the retirement of performing animals.

Countries like Bolivia, India, and Greece have outlawed the use of animals in circuses altogether. In the United States, organizations such as the American Humane Association oversee animal welfare on film sets, while other advocacy groups call for the end of all animal actors, arguing that CGI can replace them entirely.

Public education and activism have also led to policy changes at major media companies. Disney, Netflix, and others now face significant pressure not to use real monkeys in productions. Animal talent agencies that previously rented out monkeys are shutting down or transitioning to educational outreach instead.

Today, many squirrel monkeys that were once performers are retired to sanctuaries, where they are given the chance to live with conspecifics in enriched environments that mimic their natural habitat.

Impact on Public Perception

The use of squirrel monkeys in science and entertainment has left a lasting mark on the public imagination. On the one hand, it introduced many people to the species and sparked interest in their conservation. On the other hand, it has fostered misconceptions and unrealistic expectations.

For example, the depiction of squirrel monkeys as cute and obedient pets in media has led to their demand in the exotic pet trade. Unfortunately, these portrayals rarely reflect the reality of their needs, intelligence, and behavioral challenges, leading many owners to surrender them or keep them in inappropriate conditions.

Scientific studies, especially those that induced psychological stress or illness, contributed to a perception of squirrel monkeys as passive tools rather than sentient beings. But as neuroscience itself has progressed, we've come to recognize their depth of feeling and social complexity.

Modern conservation campaigns often focus on educating the public about the true nature of squirrel monkeys—playful, social, and intelligent animals that belong in the wild or in large, enriched environments, not cages or movie sets.

Moving Forward: Advocacy, Education, and Reform

The future of squirrel monkeys in research and entertainment hinges on ethical progress, policy reform, and public awareness. Fortunately, the trajectory is promising.

Numerous sanctuaries and organizations now exist to rescue and rehabilitate squirrel monkeys formerly used in laboratories or shows. These include Primarily Primates in Texas, Jungle Friends in Florida, and the Monkey Sanctuary in the UK. These centers provide lifelong care and advocate for legislation to protect primates from exploitation.

Educational institutions increasingly rely on non-invasive observation or virtual reality models to study squirrel monkey behavior, emphasizing respect and learning over manipulation.

Rehabilitation programs now highlight the cognitive enrichment needs of monkeys, including puzzle feeders, social grouping, and naturalistic habitat structures. Training and caretaking protocols now prioritize positive reinforcement over coercion, minimizing stress and maximizing well-being.

The public, too, plays a role. By rejecting entertainment that exploits animals, supporting sanctuaries and conservation programs, and spreading accurate information, we collectively move toward a world where squirrel monkeys are appreciated rather than used.

Conclusion

The story of squirrel monkeys in research and entertainment is complex—a mixture of scientific progress, human fascination, and ethical reckoning. While they have contributed to valuable discoveries and brought joy to many, the costs to their welfare have been significant. As our understanding of animal cognition, emotion, and rights continues to evolve, so must our actions.

Rather than subjects or spectacles, squirrel monkeys deserve to be seen as what they truly are: intelligent, feeling beings with rich inner lives and vital roles in their native ecosystems. The time has come to replace curiosity with compassion, and fascination with responsibility. Through advocacy, education, and respect, we can honor their legacy—not by keeping them in cages, but by ensuring their freedom, health, and dignity.

CHAPTER 14:

CONSERVATION AND THE WILD POPULATION

Squirrel monkeys, with their expressive eyes, agile movements, and highly social behaviors, captivate the hearts of animal lovers and wildlife enthusiasts across the globe. Yet, behind their charming demeanor lies a harsh reality: their natural populations are increasingly vulnerable to a variety of human-induced threats. As deforestation intensifies, illegal wildlife trade flourishes, and human encroachment continues, squirrel monkeys are facing numerous challenges that endanger their long-term survival. This chapter explores the threats squirrel monkeys face in the wild, ongoing conservation efforts, and the important role pet owners and the broader public can play in protecting these fascinating primates.

Threats in the Wild: Deforestation, Poaching, and Illegal Trade

The most pressing threat to wild squirrel monkey populations is habitat loss. These monkeys are native to Central and South America, inhabiting tropical rainforests, lowland swamps, and riverside woodlands. However, extensive deforestation driven by agricultural expansion, cattle ranching, urban development, and logging has decimated large portions of their native environments. When trees are cut down, squirrel monkeys not only lose their shelter but also their food sources, which include fruits, insects, and small animals found in the dense canopy.

In some regions, logging is conducted illegally, and protected lands are invaded by developers or miners seeking natural resources. This destruction fragments habitats, forcing squirrel monkeys into smaller, isolated pockets of forest. In fragmented habitats, monkey troops may face increased stress, reduced genetic diversity due to inbreeding, and elevated risks of predation or competition with other species. Fragmentation also disrupts their foraging behavior, making survival more difficult.

Another serious threat is poaching and illegal wildlife trade. Squirrel monkeys are often captured from the wild to supply the exotic pet industry, or sold for use in medical research. Poachers frequently use cruel and inhumane methods to trap them, often killing mothers to steal their infants. Young monkeys endure great stress when taken from their social groups, and many do not survive the journey to market due to poor handling and transport conditions.

Beyond the pet trade, some squirrel monkeys fall victim to traditional beliefs or are hunted for bushmeat. Although they are not a primary food source in many regions, they are occasionally killed when food is scarce or as part of cultural traditions. These cumulative pressures have a serious impact on population numbers and genetic health.

Climate change, while less immediately visible, poses a long-term threat. Changes in rainfall patterns, temperature, and vegetation distribution could transform the delicate ecosystems squirrel monkeys rely upon, reducing the availability of fruiting trees and increasing the frequency of natural disasters like droughts and wildfires.

Conservation Programs and Protected Areas

Despite the growing threats, conservationists and researchers around the world are actively working to protect squirrel monkeys and their habitats. Many countries where squirrel monkeys are native, such as Brazil, Peru, Colombia, and Ecuador, have established national parks and reserves that serve as sanctuaries for primates and other endangered wildlife. These protected areas are critical, not only for providing safe habitats but also for facilitating long-term ecological research.

One notable example is the Manu National Park in Peru, which is home to several species of squirrel monkeys and a hotspot for biodiversity. Researchers in this park conduct ecological studies, monitor population dynamics, and investigate the effects of human encroachment. Their findings often inform conservation strategies and land management policies.

Several NGOs and international conservation organizations, including the World Wildlife Fund (WWF), International Union for Conservation of Nature (IUCN), and Wildlife Conservation Society (WCS), have made primate conservation a priority. These groups focus on habitat preservation, public education, and the enforcement of wildlife protection laws. Some also help local governments strengthen their anti-poaching efforts and regulate illegal wildlife trafficking routes.

Captive breeding programs, though not always ideal for primates, have been initiated in some zoological institutions to maintain genetic diversity and educate the public. Accredited zoos may collaborate to create species survival plans that ensure the long-term health of captive squirrel monkey populations, with the possibility of future reintroduction into the wild under the right circumstances.

Reforestation efforts and sustainable land-use practices are becoming increasingly important in conservation. NGOs and local governments work with indigenous communities and farmers to plant native trees, implement agroforestry techniques, and create wildlife corridors that reconnect fragmented habitats. These efforts not only benefit squirrel monkeys but also countless other species that depend on intact forests.

Community-based conservation has proven to be one of the most effective models for protecting squirrel monkeys. When local communities are involved in conservation projects and benefit from eco-tourism, education, or sustainable agriculture, they are more likely to protect the natural habitats around them. Empowering people with knowledge and resources helps to create guardians of the forest rather than exploiters.

How Pet Owners Can Support Wild Populations

Squirrel monkey enthusiasts who keep these primates in captivity—either as pets or in private facilities—have a responsibility to ensure their interest in these animals contributes to their protection rather than their decline. Pet owners can support wild squirrel monkey populations in several meaningful ways.

First and foremost, they should avoid contributing to the illegal wildlife trade. Always acquire animals from ethical, legally operating sources that can verify captive-breeding practices. Supporting reputable breeders and sanctuaries helps reduce the demand for wild-caught monkeys and discourages poaching.

Pet owners can also become ambassadors for the species by educating others about the challenges squirrel monkeys face in the wild. Sharing accurate information through social media, blogs, or public talks can raise awareness about conservation issues. Many people are unaware of the threats squirrel monkeys endure, and education can inspire them to act responsibly and support conservation efforts.

Another impactful way to support conservation is to contribute financially to organizations engaged in squirrel monkey protection. Donations help fund habitat restoration, research, anti-poaching patrols, and educational outreach. Even small recurring donations can have a cumulative impact over time.

Volunteering is another option for those who want to do more than give money. Many primate rescue centers, rehabilitation facilities, and conservation nonprofits offer volunteer programs. Participants may assist with animal care, habitat maintenance, community education, or field research. Such opportunities not only benefit the monkeys but also provide volunteers with firsthand knowledge and a deepened sense of connection.

For those who cannot volunteer directly, becoming a citizen scientist is another avenue. Some conservation organizations conduct population monitoring and environmental surveys that welcome input from the public. Photographing and logging sightings of squirrel monkeys during eco-tourism trips, for example, can contribute to biodiversity databases that help researchers understand population trends.

Pet owners can also promote responsible eco-tourism. When traveling to regions where squirrel monkeys live, choose tour operators that practice sustainable and ethical wildlife viewing. Avoid activities that involve direct contact with wild primates or that exploit animals for entertainment. Supporting local guides who value conservation helps create a market for ethical tourism and reinforces positive behavior within the local economy.

Symbolic Adoptions and Education Campaigns

Symbolic adoptions offer an accessible and meaningful way for individuals to support squirrel monkey conservation without physically caring for an animal.

Many wildlife organizations run symbolic adoption programs that allow people to "adopt" a monkey by making a financial contribution. In return, they often receive an adoption certificate, photo, and information about the species or specific monkey they are supporting. These programs help fund rescue operations, medical care, food, and habitat restoration for monkeys in need.

Symbolic adoptions are especially effective for involving children, students, or families in conservation. They can also make thoughtful gifts that spread awareness and encourage environmentally conscious behavior. Schools and community groups may adopt monkeys as part of educational projects, deepening students' understanding of ecology and ethics.

Education campaigns aimed at reducing demand for exotic pets, bushmeat, and wildlife entertainment play a crucial role in changing public perceptions. Many conservation groups develop targeted outreach programs in countries where squirrel monkeys are native, using posters, radio broadcasts, and workshops to communicate the value of preserving wildlife.

Globally, social media has become an important platform for conservation messaging. Photos and videos that showcase the beauty of wild squirrel monkeys—alongside messages about the threats they face—can reach large audiences and inspire action. The use of hashtags and viral campaigns helps create momentum and community around primate protection.

Public pressure on governments and corporations also plays a role. When consumers demand sustainable products, stronger environmental protections, and stricter enforcement of anti-trafficking laws, policymakers are more likely to act. Signing petitions, writing to representatives, and voting for eco-friendly legislation can contribute to systemic change.

Conclusion

The plight of squirrel monkeys in the wild is a sobering reminder that even the most agile and intelligent creatures are not immune to the consequences of human activity. Yet there is hope. Through international cooperation, scientific research, public education, and grassroots advocacy, we have the tools to protect these charismatic primates and ensure they continue to thrive in their natural habitats.

Whether you're a pet owner, conservationist, teacher, or student, you can make a difference. Your choices—where you donate, how you educate, what you consume, and how you advocate—ripple outward, affecting the future of the species. By taking responsibility and acting with compassion, we can help restore balance between humans and the wild, giving squirrel monkeys the chance to live freely and flourish for generations to come.

CHAPTER 15:

RESOURCES AND NEXT STEPS

Welcoming a squirrel monkey into your life is not just an act of companionship—it's a long-term commitment that requires ongoing education, a supportive community, and a deep dedication to animal welfare. The journey of learning about squirrel monkeys does not end with this book; rather, it is the beginning of a continuous path of discovery, responsibility, and advocacy. In this chapter, we explore key resources and networks that can support you in becoming a more informed and compassionate caregiver, while also highlighting broader avenues for involvement in primate conservation and education.

The Value of Continued Learning

The complexity of squirrel monkey care means that even experienced keepers must stay updated with the latest findings in primatology, veterinary medicine, enrichment strategies, and legal regulations. New studies emerge regularly that provide fresh insights into primate nutrition, behavior, and health—so maintaining a spirit of curiosity and openness to learning is essential.

Books, online platforms, peer-reviewed journals, and educational videos are all powerful tools in a keeper's knowledge arsenal. Whether you are a novice considering your first primate companion or a seasoned keeper looking to refine your methods, these resources can enhance your understanding and ensure your monkey thrives in a captive environment.

Recommended Books

Several books on primate care, behavior, and conservation can offer foundational and advanced knowledge to supplement your experience. While few books are dedicated solely to squirrel monkeys, texts on New World monkeys or general primate behavior often include valuable sections on the Saimiri genus.

Books that cover primate enrichment and training techniques are especially helpful. Look for works by veterinarians, primatologists, and zookeepers who specialize in New World monkeys or exotic pets. Topics may range from psychological stimulation and habitat design to ethical considerations and legalities.

Additionally, scientific texts and field guides offer deeper insights into squirrel monkey behavior in the wild, which is crucial for providing them with an environment that meets their species-specific needs.

Reliable Websites and Online Guides

The internet is an abundant source of information—yet not all of it is trustworthy. When seeking guidance online, it's important to distinguish between anecdotal blogs and well-researched, evidence-based platforms.

Reputable websites managed by veterinary institutions, zoological organizations, or exotic animal welfare groups often provide up-to-date content written by professionals.

These sites often include downloadable care sheets, nutritional guidelines, habitat setup recommendations, and articles on health and behavioral management. A few may even host webinars or virtual seminars where participants can interact with experts directly.

Forums and community-run websites also have value, especially when it comes to practical day-to-day care experiences. While they should never replace professional veterinary advice, these platforms can offer useful insights and emotional support from other primate keepers.

Online Forums and Social Media Groups

Connecting with other squirrel monkey owners can be one of the most enriching and informative aspects of your journey. Online forums, Facebook groups, Reddit communities, and specialized primate care discussion boards offer opportunities to exchange advice, share experiences, and ask questions.

These communities often include breeders, rescue workers, veterinarians, and long-time owners who are happy to lend their wisdom to others. They may share photos of enrichment setups, feeding techniques, or success stories that help you see your own monkey's care in a new light.

Of course, it is essential to maintain a critical eye when reading online advice. Always verify health- or behavior-related claims with a qualified veterinarian or primate expert, and be cautious of any posts promoting unregulated or illegal sales of exotic animals.

Organizations for Primate Welfare and Advocacy

There are several nonprofit organizations and sanctuaries around the world dedicated to the welfare of primates—

both in captivity and in the wild. These organizations often work to rescue primates from abusive or inappropriate situations, provide lifelong sanctuary, campaign against illegal wildlife trade, and conduct public education campaigns.

Supporting these organizations can take many forms. Some welcome volunteers or allow virtual participation in conservation initiatives. Others offer newsletters, courses, and webinars to inform and empower people who care for primates. Many depend on donations and public support to carry out their missions.

As a squirrel monkey owner or enthusiast, aligning with these groups can reinforce your commitment to ethical care. It also connects you to a broader mission that transcends personal ownership—contributing to the global effort to protect and preserve squirrel monkeys and other primates.

Connecting with Sanctuaries and Rehabilitation Centers

Even if you do not intend to adopt a squirrel monkey from a sanctuary, establishing a relationship with one can be tremendously helpful. These organizations are often staffed with individuals who have decades of experience with primates and can offer guidance, mentorship, and even emergency advice.

Visiting a sanctuary—where permitted—can also be an eye-opening experience. It offers a chance to observe primates in environments designed to replicate their natural habitats and learn how professionals manage group dynamics, enrichment, and behavioral issues.

Furthermore, fostering relationships with these institutions may help you in times of personal transition. If, for any reason, you are no longer able to care for your squirrel monkey, having trusted contacts at reputable sanctuaries can help ensure your animal continues to receive the care it needs.

Continuing Education and Certification Programs

For those who want to take their understanding even further, various institutions offer continuing education programs focused on exotic animal care. Universities, veterinary colleges, and wildlife conservation groups may offer short courses or full certification programs that touch on primate physiology, disease prevention, behavioral psychology, and nutrition.

Many of these courses are available online and are designed for flexible learning. They are suitable for hobbyists, aspiring zookeepers, or animal welfare professionals. These programs can also improve your credibility and deepen your knowledge when engaging with other professionals or pet communities.

Some courses may include interactive sessions, where participants can pose questions to primatologists, veterinarians, or behaviorists. Certificates earned from these programs may be useful if you're applying for permits or want to volunteer with reputable wildlife organizations.

Advocating for Better Primate Care

As a squirrel monkey owner or advocate, you are in a unique position to shape how others perceive and treat these animals. Advocacy begins with education—sharing correct information, dispelling myths, and promoting ethical care standards. Whether through blogging, public speaking, or social media engagement, your voice can help shift attitudes and practices in the exotic pet community.

Advocacy may also involve lobbying for better laws and regulations concerning exotic animal trade, transportation, and captivity. Many regions still lack robust policies to prevent abuse, overbreeding, and neglect. Supporting legislation or raising awareness of these gaps can lead to long-term improvements in primate welfare.

Another impactful way to advocate is through symbolic adoption or sponsorship programs offered by primate sanctuaries. These initiatives allow you to support the care of squirrel monkeys without keeping them as pets. They also provide educational materials that can be shared with others to spark interest and compassion.

Building a Legacy of Compassion

Your commitment to a squirrel monkey's welfare can extend far beyond the animal in your care. Through responsible ownership, education, and advocacy, you become a model for others who may be interested in exotic pets. The choices you make—whether it's sourcing from ethical breeders, providing exemplary care, or speaking out on primate welfare issues—help set higher standards for everyone.

By nurturing a network of like-minded individuals and organizations, you strengthen your capacity to make informed, ethical decisions. You also contribute to a more compassionate world where primates are respected, protected, and allowed to thrive, whether in a responsible captive setting or their native habitat.

Final Thoughts

The journey with squirrel monkeys is unlike any other. These highly intelligent, social, and sensitive beings deserve a life filled with respect, enrichment, and care tailored to their complex needs. The road ahead will be filled with joys, challenges, and constant learning, but you are never alone in this endeavor.

Use the resources available to you. Lean into the wisdom of professionals and fellow enthusiasts. Stay informed, stay compassionate, and never stop advocating for better lives—for your monkey and for all primates.

Your next steps could be as simple as joining a primate care forum, subscribing to a sanctuary's newsletter, or attending an online seminar. Whatever action you choose, let it be rooted in empathy, responsibility, and a genuine desire to do right by these remarkable animals.

In supporting their well-being, you will find yourself transformed—more patient, more observant, and deeply connected to a species whose future now, in some small but significant way, rests in your hands.

Made in the USA
Monee, IL
18 September 2025